THE
REAGAN
PERSUASION

CHARM, INSPIRE, AND DELIVER
A WINNING MESSAGE

JAMES C. HUMES

sourcebooks

Published by Sourcebooks, Inc.
P.O. Box 4410, Naperville, Illinois 60567-4410
(630) 961-3900
Fax: (630) 961-2168
www.sourcebooks.com

Library of Congress Cataloging-in-Publication Data

Humes, James C.
   The Reagan Persuasion : charm, inspire, and deliver a winning message /
James C. Humes.
      p. cm.
   1. Reagan, Ronald--Oratory. 2. Reagan, Ronald--Language. 3. Rhetoric--
Political aspects--United States--History--20th century. 4. Communication in
politics--United States--History--20th century. 5. English language--United
States--Rhetoric. 6. Public speaking--Handbooks, manuals, etc. I. Title.
   E877.2.H86 2009
   973.927092--dc22

                         2008041757

         Printed and bound in the United States of America.
              VP 10 9 8 7 6 5 4 3 2 1

DEDICATION

★ ★ ★ ★ ★

To my daughter, Rachel Bailey Humes, who attended the first inaugural ceremony of Ronald Reagan with me in January 1981 in Washington, where afterward we feasted on Belgian pancakes in the new Reagan White House.

TABLE OF CONTENTS

★ ★ ★ ★ ★

ACKNOWLEDGMENTS

★ ★ ★ ★ ★

Again, my thanks to Linda Graham, who transmitted my handwriting into manuscript form with constructive comments and suggestions, and to Barbara Veylupek, for her assistance. I also had assistance from Susy Brandt.

I appreciate the efforts of my literary agent, Carol Mann, in a flat book market.

Hillel Black, my editor, made helpful and constructive comments that shaped and improved the manuscript.

Finally, I have to thank Steve Schuck of the Schuck Foundation and its president, Don Griffin, whose support makes possible my writing and lecturing.

THE FIFTEEN SECRETS OF
THE GREAT COMMUNICATOR

★ ★ ★ ★ ★

Ronald Reagan was more than just "the Great Communicator." He was the giant political personality of our time. No one would call Reagan a political philosopher, least of all himself. But Reagan would profoundly reshape the political dialogue in America. Just as his early hero Franklin Roosevelt made liberalism the dominant American political philosophy, a half-century later Reagan would make the majority of his country's citizens accept conservatism as their worldview. But, if Franklin Roosevelt promised more government as the solution to society ills, Reagan would say the government was "not the solution but part of the problem." Reagan, like Teddy Roosevelt, found the White House "a bully pulpit" for promoting his views and persuading Americans to adopt them.

"WON THE WAR WITHOUT
FIRING A SHOT"

British Prime Minister Margaret Thatcher said of Reagan, "He won the Cold War without firing a shot." Certainly the U.S.'s overwhelming superiority in nuclear defense systems played an important part. But as powerful as the weaponry were Reagan's words. When most of our academic experts on the USSR, including those of our State Department as well as the British Foreign Office, projected the continuation of the Soviet Empire and the Cold War for at least two more decades, Reagan prophesized to the British Parliament an earlier date for its collapse. Reagan asserted: "Marxism is on the ash heap of history." That phrase resonated in the Soviet satellite countries east of the Iron Curtain, and countries like Poland responded to Reagan's challenge.

SELLER OF THE FREE MARKET TO THE FREE WORLD

For decades, American presidents had shrunk back from praising the virtues of capitalism. To say something positive about the profit incentive was like defending millionaires. In speaking in Western Europe, where just about all of the countries had socialist or social democratic governments, American presidents had shied away from lauding the "profit motive" as a key to economic growth. Profit was to many a euphemism for greed. Reagan was the first president to proclaim the greatness of the free market society, as well as freedom. Rather than echoing the defensiveness of previous presidents, he mounted an offensive on behalf of capitalism.

"MR. GORBACHEV, TEAR DOWN THIS WALL!"

The citizens of East Germany, also known as the German Democratic Republic, were altogether painfully aware of the different standards of living on both sides of the Iron Curtain, and proved to be a receptive audience. When Reagan pointed out there was no record of any West Germans climbing the Wall to go into East Germany, or of any Austrians trying to cross into Hungary, his message filtered into Eastern Europe, triggering a rising wave of protests that began in Poland. Reagan's words spread the seeds of counterrevolution. His demand to the Soviet leader in Berlin, "Mr. Gorbachev, tear down this wall," would be the rallying call for East Germans a decade after he proclaimed that communism was on the "ash heap of history."

Readers need to be reminded that before Reagan entered the White House in 1981, Republicans had not controlled the House in Congress since 1954 or the Senate since 1956. Most of the big, populous eastern states were dominated by Democrats, and so was much of the rural south. The Democrats were the overwhelming majority party.

In 1981, when the Democratic House of Representatives, led by Speaker Tip O'Neill, opposed President Reagan's tax cutting reforms, as well as his call for deregulation, Reagan went over the head of Congress by appealing in his speeches to the American people, and his programs of cutting taxes and red tape prevailed.

GREAT PERSUADER

Reagan was not only "the Great Communicator" but he was also the Great Persuader. Lord Bryce, author of *The American Commonwealth*, wrote in 1908, "The great president would be one who could both stir audiences at the stump, as well as sway members of the caucus." In other words, he could sell to mass audiences, as well as one-on-one. Reagan won hearts and minds in his private conversations and in his public addresses, as well. His affability and choice of words melted the potential hostilities of adversaries and created a relaxed atmosphere for an exchange of views. He made it seem effortless and not strained, but he prepared for those meetings with sedulous care.

SECRETS OF REAGAN

No advice on speech could ever make you a clone of Ronald Reagan. As Lady Thatcher told this writer in October 2007 in the House of Lords, "James, they threw away the mold when they made Ronald Reagan." But you can learn Reagan's secrets of style, presence, and flair, as well as his techniques for making a talk powerful and persuasive.

This book is not just for wannabe CEOs—middle-management types who wish to polish and perfect their presentations and advance up the corporate ladder. This is for anyone who is ever called upon to make a talk—whether it be a presentation to the local PTA, a toast or tribute at a retirement dinner, or an introduction of a visiting speaker at a service club luncheon. Every time you stand at the podium, you are doing a casting call for a leadership role. Every time you have to deliver a talk to a neighborhood volunteer group or to a trade association or to the chamber of commerce, you are looked upon as a leader. So you had better live up to it!

You may not ever run for president, but if you follow the tips in this book, don't be surprised if you find yourself being asked to run a charitable drive, the campaign for a voters' referendum, or even a company.

Think of how winning your presentations are going to be when you learn Reagan's secrets of crafting the self-deprecating one-liner to make yourself likeable, or coining the memorable zinger line, or ending with a poignant anecdote or ringing challenge that will bring an audience to its feet. If you want to speak like Reagan, all you have to do is learn his secrets!

CHAPTER I

PREPARATION IS PARAMOUNT

★ ★ ★ ★ ★

A former president for whom I once drafted a speech looked at it for the first time only as he was descending in a hotel elevator in Greenwich, Connecticut, to address a Republican fund-raising rally. Reagan would, however, have read and reread again the draft while ever editing the wording for better edge, lilt, and rhythm. In fact, no president ever delivered an address or talk better prepared.

"ONE-SHOT RON"

White House speechwriters used to say that Nixon edited for substance and Reagan for style, but both Ford and Bush (41) hardly changed a word. Reagan not only polished style but practiced delivery. He had always thoroughly mastered the text before he stepped to the podium. In Hollywood, directors called him "One-Shot Ron." In all of his thirty-six movies, there was never one retake on his lines. (He did have to dive into a tank of icy water sixteen times for a film with Shirley Temple, but that was to master an action shot, not a dialogue line.)

In 1946, Reagan played a soldier named Yank in a supporting role to Richard Todd in *The Hasty Heart*. In one scene, taking place in an English war hospital, the Brit [Todd] claimed that the Yank [Reagan] doesn't know his Bible. Reagan, as Yank, proceeded to reel off every book of the Bible—"Genesis, Exodus, Leviticus, Numbers, Deuteronomy, Lamentations...," all the way through to the last—Revelation. The witnessing technicians and camera crew cheered at Reagan's faultless rendition that didn't need a retake.

Most attribute Reagan's success as a speaker to his career as an actor. It is true that his years as an actor had developed his memory and honed his sense of timing, but he taught himself the art of presence.

In fact, most film actors and actresses are not accomplished speakers, with the exception of those who were once stage actors skilled at delivering long speeches like Shakespearean soliloquies—Laurence Olivier and Richard Burton, for example. Movie actors are used to delivering just a line or two—not a speech—as this writer found out when he wrote drafts of speeches for Senator George Murphy, Shirley Temple, and Cary Grant. Grant, for example, was terrified of delivering a set speech. Instead, I prepared a series of snappy one-liners in response to questions from women in the hall or auditorium. He would open by saying, "You are such beautiful women, I am going to tear up this speech [he would tear it up] and just answer some of your questions like old friends."

GREATEST SPEECHWRITER IN THE WHITE HOUSE SINCE LINCOLN

Reagan became the most in-demand popular banquet speaker in America. In delivering those thousands of talks, he had developed his writing skills and perfected the art of delivery. The fact is that the greatest speechwriter in the White House since Abraham Lincoln was Ronald Reagan.

Lincoln had honed his skills as a lawyer appealing to juries in order to win huge awards against train companies that had run over his clients' cows. This writer, who also addressed juries when he was a young lawyer, knows how he used to work in some of his favorite lines again and again in closing appeals to jury members. A speechwriter gains a feel for which lines are most effective and knows how to deliver them best.

Reagan wrote all of his talks when he was on the national speaking circuit, and he knew through audience reactions which lines were winners. Think back to your own experiences. There are certain stories that you have told again and again, such as how you met your significant other: "I never liked redheads, and there she came in with those green eyes and that emerald dress." Or maybe it's a self-deprecating tale: "At the end of the high school football game, I threw the deciding pass—it was going for a winning touchdown, only it was the other team that made the touchdown after they intercepted it." Or: "I had picked out this smashing gown for the senior prom, only to find the class beauty was wearing the same gown."

You have told the stories so many times you know just when to pause before a significant word or just when to lower your voice.

Reagan had delivered both his "parables," or stories, and his "zinger" lines hundreds of times, and his speeches never failed to win standing ovations. The secret of Reagan's success was that he looked natural at the podium. The lines did not seem rehearsed.

CONVERSATIONAL, NOT ORATORICAL

Reagan was like the woman who spends two hours applying her makeup to make it appear as if she has no makeup on at all. Reagan may not have read the Athenian's criticism of the orator Demosthenes that his speeches "smelled too much of the lamp"—that is, suffered from too much overwriting—but Reagan never overwrote. Reagan did not approve of Sorensen's crafted line for JFK's inaugural address in that [Demosthenes] category—

"Ask not what your country can do for you…" To Reagan it was oratorical, not conversational.

Reagan told this writer that he would sacrifice "quotability" for "credibility." When drafting his talks, he imagined himself speaking to his barber in Santa Barbara. Reagan would not say to the barber or to a friend over drinks such oratorical lines, however beautiful or memorable. White House speechwriter Ray Price once crafted for Nixon this line: "Faith may move mountains, but faith without strength is futile, but strength without faith is sterile." It may be laden with alliteration and rhyme, but it does not sound conversational.

NEITHER PREACH NOR PONTIFICATE

A long-time Congressional colleague, friend, and supporter of Al Gore complained to this writer that Gore would pontificate in private conversation—and he did in public speeches too. Reagan, in his speeches, was speaking to everyone in the audience as if having a conversation at the kitchen table rather than preaching from a pulpit. Reagan, who read the *Autobiography of Benjamin Franklin*, marveled at his simple, conversational language. In the eighteenth century, the style was formal and ornate. Reagan also took note that Franklin disapproved of phrases—such as "Anyone knows…" or

"Of course, it's obvious that..."—that are condescending and patronizing, which is how Gore and his fellow Democratic candidate John Kerry often sounded.

NO BLOVIATING

Reagan also had disdain for those rhetorical tricks Athenian orators invented to underscore a key line. At FDR's first inaugural address, he opened with his most-quoted line, "Let me again assert my firm belief that the only thing we have to fear is fear itself." The opening phrase is inserted to emphasize what comes after to make reporters repeat it in their next day's story. It was like Nixon saying, "Let me be perfectly clear..." Such phrasing actually undercuts the sincerity you want to project instead of enforcing it. Kennedy, in the middle of his inaugural address, said, "And so, my fellow Americans: ask not what your country can do..." Reagan's reaction: "It's in the middle of his Inaugural address. Who was he speaking to—Germans?" To Reagan, such words smacked of a state senator bloviating at a county fair. "And ladies and gentleman, I say to you..."

NO SPEECHWRITER

From his acting days, Reagan knew a line of dialogue had to sound natural and conversational, yet carry a certain bite and thrust. Reagan had long experience in coining ringing lines that sounded conversational. It started in his scripts for his radio career before he went to Hollywood. When his movie career faded, it continued when he became a spokesman for General Electric, which sponsored his "Tales of the West" on TV. His talks to GE employees in plants across the nation were the prelude to his becoming the top speaker in the country during the Eisenhower years. He employed no speechwriter. He drafted his own remarks. Those seated next to Reagan at the head table used to report seeing no text before him—only a few notes.

They assumed, that is, that there was no written speech, much like onlookers reported that Lincoln drafted his Gettysburg Address on the back of the envelope on a train. (Actually, Lincoln had already written six drafts of the Gettysburg Address. The notes on the envelope were key words in the speech written in succession as a rehearsing and memory aid.) Reagan did the same thing—writing and revising the full text well in advance, but using only notes of major phrases to work from on the platform. If Lincoln was the greatest White House speechwriter, Reagan was the second greatest.

PARABLE FIRST

As the date of each speech would loom, Reagan would collect his thoughts and begin jotting down some notes, first considering the kind of audience he would be speaking to and the message he wanted to leave with that audience. A speech to a national trade association would be different than one to a World Affairs Council event in Philadelphia. He'd begin the speech by choosing an anecdote from his files. To a business group, it would be something that poked fun of big government bureaucracy. To an international affairs organization, it might be a parody of the failure of communism.

SECOND, THE CLOSER

Then he would contemplate how he would end it on a high inspirational note—maybe a vignette from American history or a poetic verse. After that he would get down to the task of writing it on paper.

Try following this formula the next time you are asked to prepare a talk, no matter how brief. First, concentrate on identifying the audience—a sales force? A trade association filled with potential clients? A local civic group? A chamber of commerce? A breakfast meeting? Prepare to tailor your message to your audience, and then consider the message itself. What is the biggest point you want to get across? The quality of your product? The right climate in which to invest? The importance of community involvement? The right product image?

Then think of a personal experience that would exemplify that message—and prove that point.

TRY OUT FOR A LEADERSHIP ROLE

Next, work on crafting a closing line or paragraph that will really lift and call your audience to action.

Remember, every time you speak, you are auditioning for a promotion. It would be wise for you to develop your own set talk, such as "Five Clues to the Commercial Real Estate Market," or "How to Set Up Your Own Company," or "Five Ways to Become a Millionaire before You're Fifty."

If you have developed one talk at which you look your winning best, insist on delivering that speech.

When you stand in front of an audience, you are trying out for a leadership role. If you adopt the methods of "the Great Communicator," you will become that leader.

CHAPTER II

THE TAKE-AWAY PARABLE

★ ★ ★ ★ ★

The greatest raconteur to ever preside as head of government was Ronald Reagan. Perhaps Winston Churchill was the greatest orator, but in storytelling, Reagan was his superior. The spinning of stories is distinctly an American trait. This tradition started in the frontier days when a rider would be put up for the night in a family's cabin. The visitor would feel that he had to "sing for his supper" in return for the meal, lodging, and stabling of his horse. In the days before magazines—not to mention radio or television—the guest who could regale his hosts with exaggerated tales of his adventures was much relished and appreciated.

STORYTELLERS

Abraham Lincoln enthralled local audiences by spinning tall tales to his fellow lawyers and others when he was riding the circuit. He continued his storytelling as president. In fact, Lincoln, like Reagan, would use storytelling as amiable armor to deflect intimacy.

FDR, who was in so many ways a model for Reagan,

had, like Lincoln, the gifts of mimicry and timing to be an entertaining raconteur with his Oval Office audiences.

Roosevelt's favorite author was Mark Twain, who was the first to commercialize his yarn-spinning talents and become the most popular and best paid speaker in the English-speaking world. (Incidentally, the only American to have more sayings than FDR cited in *Bartlett's Familiar Quotations* was Mark Twain.) And Reagan was a fan of Benjamin Franklin, whose storytelling kept his fellow delegates at the Constitutional Convention rapt, just as he had managed to do in the Court of Louis XVI in Versailles. Storytelling was as much a part of the American fabric as the plain muslin broadcloth shirts that Franklin wore to the satin-and-silk courtiers at Versailles.

British politicians, because of their debating experience in Parliament, may have developed skills superior to their American counterparts in repartee, the witty turn-of-phrase, and the clever rejoinder. Their Parliamentary records, however, reveal no stories, while American politicians, like Senators Sam Ervin or Everett Dirksen, fill the Congressional Record with their own tales.

In the first chapter, we discussed that the first thing Reagan would figure out as he prepared for his next speech appearance was which story he would tell. This was no small task. Reagan's son, Michael, told this writer that he found in Reagan's desk at the ranch in Santa Barbara a thousand stories compressed into a few notes on 3 by 5 cards. They were labeled with titles such as "Manure under the Christmas Tree" or "The Oldest Profession." Reagan would flip through the cards until he found one that would be appropriate for the talk at hand.

For Reagan, the story he selected had to meet two criteria: it had to entertain, and it had to exemplify the major message of his address.

"THE LITTLE RED HEN"

In his days on the circuit in the 1950s, Reagan was frequently invited as a speaker to the annual meeting of business trade associations. For these groups, he often used an anecdote he had labeled "The Modern Little Red Hen."

> *Once upon a time, there was a little red hen who scratched around the barnyard until she discovered some grains of wheat. She called her neighbors and said, "If we plant this wheat, we shall have bread to eat. Who will help me reap my wheat?"*
>
> *"Not I," said the duck.*
>
> *"Out of my classification," said the pig.*
>
> *"I'd lose my seniority," said the cow.*
>
> *"Then I will," said the little red hen; and she did.*

At last it came time to bake the bread.

"Who will help me bake the bread?" asked the little red hen.

"That will be overtime for me," said the cow.

"I'd lose my welfare benefits," said the duck.

"I'm a dropout and never learned how," said the pig.

"If I'm only to be a helper, that's discrimination," said the goose.

"Then I will," said the little red hen.

She baked five loaves and held them up for neighbors to see. They all wanted some and, in fact, demanded a share. But the little red hen said, "No. I can eat the five loaves myself."

"Excess profit," said the cow.

"Capitalist leech," screamed the duck.

"I demand equal rights," yelled the goose.

And they all painted picket signs and marched around the little red hen, shouting obscenities. When the government agent came, he said to the little red hen, "You must not be so greedy."

"But I earned the bread," she said.

"Exactly," said the agent. "That's the wonderful free enterprise system. Anyone in the barn can earn as much as he wants, but under our modern government regulations, the productive workers must divide their product with the idle."

> *And they lived happily ever after. But her barn neigh-*
> *bors complained that she never baked any more bread.*

Reagan loved parables, and this was a favorite of his. Yes, it brought a chuckle, but more importantly, it enforced an economic truth.

THE PRODIGAL SON

Reagan's mother would take him and his brother, "Moon," to the Christian Church every Sunday in Dixon. It was there that young Reagan came to appreciate the force of parables that Jesus told. Jesus was a master storyteller. Jesus concocted the parable of the prodigal son to show the forgiveness of God for a sinner. Jesus was a master at emulating the rabbinical technique of illustrating the principles of the Talmud with examples and stories. And a large part of his success was due to the fact that he never forgot that he was talking to shepherds and fishermen. If Jesus had used Paul's Greek word "salvation," they would not have understood him, but his tale of the prodigal son entertained, as well as enlightened, his audience. To illustrate the notion of humanity, Jesus told the story of the Good Samaritan. For years to come, the gist of those sermons would be repeated by illiterate fishermen and shepherds until one day they retold those parables to the men who were writing the New Testament. Talk about the power of the take-away parable!

PARABLES WITH A POINT

To a Republican group shortly after he was inaugurated in 1981, Reagan illustrated the magnitude of the job facing him after the Democratic Congress had ruled the country for close to three decades. Reagan recalled his play-by-play days as an announcer in Des Moines, Illinois, for the Chicago Cubs.

> *One day against the Cubs, the great and future Hall of Fame Cardinal manager, Frankie Frisch, sent a rookie out to play centerfield. The rookie promptly dropped the first fly ball that was hit to him. On the next play, he let a grounder go through his legs, and then he threw the ball to the wrong base.*
>
> *Frankie stormed out to centerfield, took the glove from him, and said, "I'll show you how to play the position." The next batter slammed a drive right over second base. Frankie came in on it, missed it completely, fell down when he tried to chase it, threw down his glove, and yelled to the rookie, "YOU'VE GOT CENTERFIELD SO SCREWED UP NOBODY CAN PLAY IT."*

On his 3 by 5 cards, the punch line would be in caps. The caption on this tale's card read "Frisch and the Rookie in CF." In between the title and the punch line would be key points rather than a narrative—in this example, "Rookie drops ball—grounder—wrong base—Frisch misses ball…"

In 1984, Reagan was scheduled to speak to a Cuban-American group in Miami. To these anti-Castroites, who had fled from communism, he told a folk story about a Soviet commissioner who went to inspect one of the collective farms.

The commissioner stopped the first farmer that he met and asked him about life on the farm. The man said, "It's wonderful. I've never heard anyone complain about anything since I've been here."

The commissioner said, "Well, what about the crops?"

"Oh," the farmer said, "the crops are wonderful."

"What about the potatoes?"

"Oh sir," he said, "the potatoes, there are so many that if we put them in one pile they would touch the foot of God."

The commissioner said, "Just a minute. In the Soviet Union there is no God."

And the farmer said, "WELL, THERE ARE NO POTATOES EITHER."

ANECDOTES ARE BETTER THAN ABSTRACTIONS

You can imagine those Cuban-Americans retelling that story to their family and friends. It is that take-away story that leaves an impression far more lasting than just talking in abstractions about "godless, atheistic communism."

PARABLES ARE PICTURES

As a spokesman for General Electric, Reagan often regaled his audiences with a parable about the farce and failure of communism. The story concerned a man who went to the Soviet Bureau of Transportation to order an automobile.

He was told to put his money down, even though there was a ten-year wait. Nevertheless, he filled out the various forms, had them processed to the various agencies, and signed his name in countless places. Finally, he got to the last agency, where they put a stamp on the papers. He gave them money, and they said, "Come back in ten years to get your car."

He asked, "Morning or afternoon?"

They said, "What difference does that make? We're talking about ten years from now."

The man answered, "YOU SEE, THE PLUMBER IS COMING IN THE MORNING."

A parable is a picture printed on the mind.

Reagan's early hero in politics was Franklin Roosevelt. Reagan told an audience from the National Association of Manufacturers this anecdote about the marriage of Franklin Roosevelt Jr., to Margaret DuPont.

> *Now here was the son of the head of the Democratic Party marrying the daughter of the biggest corporate chief in capitalism. Naturally, the gods were offended, and cloudbursts fell upon the reception visitors in Wilmington, Delaware. A reporter asked, "Mr. President, does the rain dampen the spirit of the occasion?"*
>
> *President Roosevelt piped back, "No, it's always a grand day when I see so many rich business types getting soaked."*

Reagan also had a special affection for Lincoln. They both lived in Illinois and shared a penchant for storytelling. Reagan collected Lincoln's anecdotes and told many of them on the speech circuit. Perhaps the one he told the most was about Lincoln and the job seeker.

I inserted this Lincoln story in a speech I was writing for a company head who wanted to stress to his stockholders the superiority of his company's market position over its chief competitor. To put it simply, he said he would hate to be in their place.

> *Abraham Lincoln was constantly besieged by office seekers who wanted to be appointed to a federal job. One day a Pennsylvanian came to his Executive Mansion. "Abe," he said. "I understand that the customs official in Philadelphia just died."*
>
> *Lincoln nodded, "That's right."*
>
> *"Well, could I take his place?"*
>
> *"Yes," replied Lincoln. "That is—if it's okay with the undertaker."*

Conversely, if you happen to be one of those executives who have to defend last year's ups and downs, you might want to borrow this tale Lincoln told of a preacher's sermon in Illinois.

PERFECTION AND THE PREACHER

> *The preacher said, "There was only one perfect person who ever lived, and that was Jesus Christ. All who believe that, raise your hands." All but one did. That was a mousy looking woman with a worn face sitting in the back.*
>
> *"Tell me, are you saying there is another perfect person?"*
>
> *"Yes," she whispered weakly.*
>
> *"Name that person," thundered the reverend.*
>
> *She answered, "MY HUSBAND'S FIRST WIFE."*

And regardless of your audience, if you want to complain about Washington, you can repeat the story Reagan told about Benjamin Franklin.

> *It seems that at a dinner in Franklin's house in Philadelphia his guests were arguing about which was the oldest profession. Dr. Benjamin Rush, the only physician among the Founding Fathers, said, "Surely it was medicine, because removing the rib from Adam to make Eve was a surgical procedure."*
>
> *Then Thomas Jefferson, the builder of Monticello, said, "No. It was the architect. After all, he brought order out of chaos."*
>
> *"You're both wrong," said Franklin. "IT WAS THE POLITICIANS, AFTER ALL, WHO CREATED THE CHAOS!"*

But use Reagan stories with care. I once heard a civic leader "talk" about the need for community involvement. He was right to tell it as if it was in his own hometown. Like poetic license, the speaker has the raconteur's right to stretch the truth and make a good story his own.

> *A tailor lived above a drugstore back in my town. The man would always boast to his customers about his three*

sons he had educated. One was an accountant, another a lawyer, and the third a doctor.

One day he called all three of them in and said, "Mama and I would like to take a trip back to the old country, and we are asking you to pay for it."

The accountant replied, "I'd like to, but we just put in a new kitchen. I'm strapped."

The lawyer also shook his head. "Poppa, we just bought a place on the shore. It's impossible."

And the doctor said, "Poppa, we just laid out a bundle for a new Chris-Craft yacht. I just can't afford it at this time"

"Boys, I never told you this before, but when your mama and I got together, I didn't have money for a ring. In fact, I didn't have the ten dollars for a marriage license."

"Poppa, no marriage license," they all screamed. "You know what that makes us?"

The tailor replied, "Yes, and cheap ones, too!"

ADOPT ANECDOTES AS YOUR OWN EXPERIENCES

Now if you are going to tell this story effectively, you should tell it as if you knew the tailor involved. And do the same with the next yarn. But as a general rule, if you have heard an anecdote before, remember it is more than likely that much of your audience has also heard it.

This writer attended a business round table in Miami, and a business executive told the listeners of going to his twentieth high school reunion.

> *Our class dunce, clad in a one-thousand-dollar Armani suit, drove up in his top-of-the-line Mercedes-Benz, and on his arm was a blonde trophy model of a wife.*
>
> *We all plied him with drinks to hear how this guy, who barely graduated, had made it so big by selling his gaskets.*
>
> *"Well," he explained, "I found this guy that I could buy them from at four dollars a piece. And then I could sell them for eight dollars. AND YOU CAN'T BEAT THAT: 4% PROFIT!"*

GET PERSONAL

Parables are stories that leave pictures etched indelibly in your mind, and they don't necessarily have to be funny to do that. Just tell stories from your own experiences.

> *A CEO of a cleaning product company told his sales force that he was in a city in the Midwest making a talk. He arrived the night before and discovered he had forgotten a shaving kit item. Seeing a supermarket across the street, he walked over to it. Of course, he had to look for his own manufactured product. After ten minutes of not finding it, he asked a clerk for help. She*

took him to the back of the store, and on the bottom row,
way below eye level, in the back rested the product.

Another young executive was warning others of the "too good to be true" claims of a product. He told of the first car he ever bought.

I went to this used-car lot, and there was a second-hand
Thunderbird that caught my eye for $650. I informed
the salesman that I did not have that kind of money. The
salesman then said, "This is just between you and me. This
is the end of the month, and if I sell one more car, I win
a trip to Las Vegas. My wife is counting on it. Don't tell
anyone what I am selling it to you for." He then whispered
in my ear, "I'll let you have it at a steal for $450." I
bought it, and three days later the transmission gave out.

EXAGGERATE, EMBELLISH, EMBROIDER

Take your own business experience or any funny happenings in your home life, like flunking an exam because you misread the question, or scheduling a poker playing date on the night of your anniversary. If you want to prove a point, exaggerate, embellish, embroider, and then practice telling it over and over. Choose an anecdote that pictures and proves the gist of your message.

In 1988, President Reagan was invited to speak at Moscow University. He thought carefully about the choice of a funny parable. He did not want to offend his host, Mikhail Gorbachev, with some tale that made a mockery of communism. Yet he wanted to obliquely attack the system. In a dig at bureaucracies, Reagan spun this folk tale about a woman who accosted a government functionary who was "chairing" a meeting in her village.

> *There is a folk legend where I come from that when a baby is born an angel comes down from heaven and kisses him on part of the body. If the angel kisses him on the hand, he becomes a handyman. If she kisses him on his forehead, he becomes a scholar. And I've been trying to figure out where the angel kissed you that you should sit there so long and do nothing.*

The Moscow students laughed uproariously.

Your speech may not be as important as Reagan's in winning the Cold War, but it is important to your career. So choose carefully in selecting a story that will be a take-away parable in the minds of your audience. The story will be remembered for long after—and so will you.

CHAPTER III

CLARION CLOSERS

★ ★ ★ ★ ★

June 6, 1984, was the fortieth anniversary of D-Day. President Reagan was invited to deliver remarks at the U.S. Ranger Monument at Pointe du Hoc, France. Pointe du Hoc is the name of the almost vertical bluffs overlooking the Normandy beach where mounted German guns had incessantly fired down on the Allied landing troops. For the D-Day landing to succeed, Rangers had to scale those cliffs and take out the big guns.

"I WILL NOT FAIL THEE NOR FORSAKE THEE"

Reagan told of the Rangers' faith in freedom and belief in God. He closed by telling a story about General Matthew Ridgway. On the eve of D-Day, Ridgway was heading the paratroopers, who would land to give back-up to the Rangers. Ridgway opened his Bible to where Joshua, before the battle of Jericho, said, "I will not fail thee or forsake thee."

So said Reagan, "Here, in this place where the West held together, let us make a vow to our dead. Let us show them by our actions that we understand what they died for.

Let our actions say to them the words for which Matthew Ridgway listened: 'I will not fail thee nor forsake thee.'"

EMOTIONAL ENDING

Reagan would always end a talk on an inspirational note. He knew that no matter how powerful or persuasive a talk, to end on a flat note would be deflating. A dull speech that ends in a dazzle gets more applause than a powerful speech that ends prosaically.

Just as in his Normandy anniversary address, Reagan often liked to draw from historical vignettes that struck in his listeners' hearts chords of love of God and country.

When the spacecraft *Challenger* exploded in January 1986, Reagan was scheduled to deliver the State of the Union address to Congress that day. The address was postponed, and Reagan, instead, addressed the nation from the Oval Office.

Reagan recalled a poem Tyrone Power had once recited. It was at a Beverly Hills reception in 1945 hosted for Power by Gary Cooper and his wife, "Rocky." They were welcoming back Power, who had been a U.S. Army Air Force pilot in World War II. At the gathering, Power recited the poem "High Flight." It had been written by an American pilot, John Magee Jr., who had been shot down over Germany in 1941. The poem had been received by his father after he received news of his son's death. (Incidentally, the senior

Magee, at the time, was rector of St. John's Episcopal across from the White House. St. John's was the church of FDR, who personally informed Magee of his son's death.)

"TO TOUCH THE FACE OF GOD"

The first and last lines of "High Flight" read, "Oh, I have slipped the surly bonds of earth / Put out my hand, and touched the face of God." So Reagan, in his tribute to the astronauts, closed with:

> *We will never forget them nor the last time*
> *we saw them this morning, as they prepared*
> *for their journey, and waved goodbye and "slipped the*
> *surly bonds of earth" to touch the face of God.*

Stories that touched on themes of God and country were Reagan's favorite endings.

In 1982, President Reagan again appealed to pride and love of country with this hospital story.

> *Not long ago, the Marine Commandant General P.J.*
> *Jones visited the hospital in Lebanon that housed those*
> *who had been injured in the recent terrorist attack. One*
> *blind Marine—swathed from head to toe in bandages—*
> *did not believe it was the top Marine general visiting*

his bedside. He reached up to the general's shoulder and counted the number of stars—one, two, three, four.

The private nodded and then signaled with his two hands for a pen and paper. Then he wrote "Semper Fi" for Semper Fideles *(always faithful).*

Reagan then closed with: "Shouldn't we always keep faith with those brave men and women?"

There are four requisite elements for a memorable speech to go down in history—great person, great occasion, great words, and great delivery. Think of Douglas MacArthur's Farewell Address to Congress in 1951, JFK's inaugural address in 1961, Dr. Martin Luther King Jr. at the Lincoln Memorial in 1963, Reagan's concession speech at the Kansas City Republican Convention in 1976.

TAKE A PAGE FROM HISTORY

The talk that you may give to the local Rotary Club or Chamber of Commerce may lack at least two ingredients of such greatness, but you can borrow greatness from some poignant moment in history, like Reagan did, to allow your talk to close on a note of inspiration. You may not hold a high office or possess a household name, and you may not be given a forum to speak on a monumental occasion. Yet, you can still attain the heights of eloquence by making sure your speech ends on a dramatic note. You can do that by borrowing from history's most poignant and patriotic moments.

When I tell my business clients to take a tip from "the Great Communicator" and end with an inspirational note, they demur by saying, "Look, I give only a few talks."

Wrong. You deliver a talk every time you make an in-house presentation or introduce a speaker for the civic club. You make a talk every time you give out an employee-of-the-month award or a retirement gift. And every time you open your mouth, your capability as a leader is judged.

CASTING CALL FOR LEADERSHIP

When the close of your presentation or pitch falls flat, your prospects for advancement fizzle. You have failed a casting call for a leadership role.

Let's say you are asked to give an award to an employee. You might want to tell this story about Winston Churchill.

> *In 1940, Churchill was pinning the Victoria Cross on a member of the Home Guard who had rescued five lives from under a burning building that had been destroyed in the Blitz. The man said, "Mr. Churchill, you honor me."*
>
> *Churchill replied, "Ah, but you are wrong. You are the one who honors me."*

"ERECTING A CATHEDRAL"

Ronald Reagan was a spokesman for General Electric before he ran for governor of California in 1966. He would offer this closing in talks to General Electric employees across America.

> *During the Middle Ages, three stonemasons were observed while working in the city of Cologne in Germany. The onlooker asked the first mason what he was doing. He looked up and answered, "I am shaping stone." The next mason was asked the same question, and he replied, "I am making a wall." But when the third mason was given the same question, he proclaimed loudly, "I am erecting a cathedral."*

To a group of GE salespeople, Reagan ended with this challenging anecdote:

> *At the turn of the last century, Sears Roebuck listed an opening for its shoe department. Shoe sales representatives looked at it and laughed. "Africa. They don't wear shoes there." But one sales representative saw it and ripped the notice off the board. "Africa," he said, "they don't wear shoes there. What an opportunity!" and off he went. "Well," said Reagan, "just because they don't have stores, sweepers, or refrigerators now, don't let that stop you."*

Ronald Reagan called Margaret Thatcher "the other woman in my life." The second-greatest British Prime Minister in history was visiting a Texas software company in 1992. She marveled over the fantastic discoveries being made in technology and ended with this:

> *When Christopher Columbus set sail in 1492, his flagship, the* Santa Maria, *carried the flag of Queen Isabella of Castille, which bore a representation of a castle with the words "Ne plus ultra" ("nothing further") under it because Spain was considered to be the farthest point west in the world. After that, the flat earth ended.*
>
> *Then when Columbus returned and reported his discoveries in the New World to the Queen, she ordered a court painter to modify the flag to remove the "ne" so that it now read "plus ultra" ("more beyond" or "something more out there").*

"Well, with new technology and more opportunities," Thatcher added, "there is more out there."

I once drafted a speech for Margaret Thatcher in 1977, when she was Leader of the Opposition. That was before she became Prime Minister in 1978. A Conservative Party speechwriter told me how she had written in the margin of a speech draft "A.G." Thinking it referred to the Attorney

General, the Conservative Party Office took it to his office to look for any constitutional questions.

They found none and asked Mrs. Thatcher about it. "Oh, it's short for Almighty God—it reminds me to add a spiritual reference because it drives the socialists crazy."

Reagan, a weekly attendant at the Christian Church in Dixon, Illinois, and Thatcher, the daughter of a Methodist Deacon, both used stories from the Bible in their talks.

A CEO who was to speak at a retirement ceremony about a much-beloved fifty-year employee cited from the Book of Kings from the Bible.

> *Some of us may remember the story of the boy Solomon who is visited by an angel. Solomon is asked, "What gift do you need to rule your country? Looks? Riches? Fame?"*
>
> *"No," he said. "Give me an understanding heart."*
>
> *Well, our honoree would be the first to say that neither great riches nor great looks were given, but we all can attest that he received an understanding heart.*

"I HAVE FOUGHT A GOOD FIGHT"

Former Governor Tom Kean, who co-chaired the 9/11 Commission, lost in his first try to be governor of New Jersey in 1979. In his concession speech, he used the deathbed words of the Apostle Paul.

In 67 AD, the Apostle Paul found himself jailed by Nero's edict in a Roman prison. The great apostle gave a Christian visitor, Onesiphorus, a message to give Paul's protégé, Timothy, who was almost like a son to him.

The note declared, "I have fought a good fight. I have finished the race. I have kept the faith."

Presidential history offers a rich lode of stories for ending a talk dramatically. Reagan, on more than one occasion, quoted the words of his fellow Illinoisan, President Lincoln, as he left Springfield for the rail journey to Washington.

I now leave, not knowing when or whether I ever will return with a task greater than that which rested upon George Washington without assistance of that Divine Being, who ever attended him. I cannot succeed. Without that assistance, I cannot fail.

DEATHBED DECLARATION

Reagan's first political hero was Franklin Roosevelt, and he wept when he heard of Roosevelt's death in April 1945. FDR had been composing his Jefferson-Jackson Day address when he slumped over dead in Warm Springs, Georgia. These words were found on the yellow legal tablet beside his hand: "The only limit to our realization of tomorrow is our doubts of today."

In tribute to his hero, Reagan would sometimes close with this in a talk to GE employees about work-saving appliances.

General Eisenhower was the first Republican whom Reagan voted for as president. In March 1969, the old soldier was dying at Walter Reed Army Medical Center in Washington. One evening he called his son John, who was staying in a suite on the floor below him, to come up.

> *When John Eisenhower entered the room, he found*
> *his father lying in an oxygen tent. "Pull me up, Johnny,"*
> *he said. "Tell them, Johnny, that I have always loved my*
> *wife. I have always loved my family. I have always loved*
> *my country, and I have always loved my God."*

Governor Reagan would attend the funeral and hear those same words, which President Nixon used to close his eulogy of Eisenhower.

Here is another Eisenhower anecdote I gave to a CEO at a ground-breaking ceremony for a new branch building.

> *In 1948, General Eisenhower bought some ground*
> *near Gettysburg, where some of his Mennonite ancestors*

had lived. The local Register of Deeds asked, "General,
you already have a house given to you as President
of Columbia. Why do you want this?" Eisenhower
answered, "I have lived on 38 Army posts. But I wanted
once to take a piece of earth and return it to God better
than I found it."

"A NEW DAY FOR AMERICA"

If Reagan was the last great American raconteur, the first
was Benjamin Franklin. One CEO headed a Philadelphia
company that had suffered reversals in the previous year but
now was bouncing back. I wrote for him one of Reagan's
favorite anecdotes about Franklin.

At the close of the Constitutional Convention in 1787,
the delegates assisted the eighty-year-old Franklin to
sign the document. As the others were signing, Franklin
pointed to the presiding chair of the convention, which
General Washington had occupied. The design on the back
of the chair showed a sun low on the horizon.

Franklin said, "Gentlemen, I have often, in the course
of this session, looked at that sun and thought perhaps it
was a setting sun. But now I know it's a rising sun, a new
day for America, a new dawn for freedom."

LIGHTING CANDLES

Reagan would advise those who intended to speak to use poignant stories from their own experience for an emotional closer. One experience that Reagan had while president would always emotionally affect him when he related it.

> *An ambassador from Poland, who had defected in 1984, called at the White House. The former diplomat had one message, "Mr. President, never let Radio Free Europe off the air. You have no idea what it means to hear the chimes of Big Ben from the BBC in London during World War II."*
>
> *Then the Pole said, "May I ask you a favor? Mr. President, would you light a candle and put it in the window tonight, for the people of Poland?"*

Right then and there, Reagan got up and went to the second floor, lit a candle, and put it in a window. When he returned, it is said that he told the former diplomat a story about George Washington, whom Reagan revered as the greatest of our presidents.

> *At Yorktown, Virginia, in 1781, General Washington, with the Polish General Kościusko at his side, accepted the*

surrender of Lord Cornwallis. The Continental Army struck up the tune "The World Turned Upside Down." Afterwards, Washington gave a fife player a penny, and said, "Go home and buy thirteen candles and light them for the thirteen new United States."

DOG STORY

The head of a pet security firm that had branches all over the world showed me the address he planned to give to all of his top executives regarding the future plans and prospects of the company. I told him his ending was flat and added, "You must have a dog story in your life."

"As a matter of fact, I do," he replied. "My first dog, Champ, I brought him home as a puppy. He more than shared my bed. He shared my life. Then one day he got out of the yard and escaped. He was found dead in the road. I think that's the first time I ever thought of forming a company that would protect the four-legged members of our family." So he ended his talk with his story about Champ, and it brought his audience to its feet.

The president of a gas safety valve company told me how his father had quit a gas valve company to develop a new type of gas safety valve. He had to work out of his own cellar. His friends all advised him to quit. They said that even if he perfected the device, the patent certification would take too long for him to benefit from the invention financially.

His son, John McGowan, Jr., said he repeated those warnings to his father. His father pointed his finger at him and said, "Son, a McGowan doesn't quit." And he got the patent.

On July 4, 1988, I represented President Reagan at a ceremony on the steps of Independence Hall in Philadelphia. In preparing my remarks, I was thinking about how to end it when my wife advised me, "Why don't you tell about the first Fourth of July you really remember?"

The first Fourth of July that I remember was 1942 in Williamsport, Pennsylvania. I was but seven years old. My father was a judge, and he took me to call on a Mrs. Knight, who had just celebrated her one-hundredth birthday.

Mrs. Knight was rocking in a chair on the front porch of her daughter's house. My father said, "Shake hands with Mrs. Knight. Her father fought in the War of Independence that we celebrate today."

Mrs. Knight said in a singsong cackle, "Yes, Papa said he wanted to go, and grandpappy said he was too young. But Papa said he could be a drummer boy (a most dangerous position that signaled when to fire the muskets). And so he was a drummer boy in 1781."

Then I told my audience, "We are the oldest continuing representative democracy, but think of this speaker as one who shook hands with someone whose father fought to forge that democracy. Let us ever honor his and others' sacrifice and service."

As Reagan once said, "You can play a special part in the future of our country. You'll be its author and take advantage of the wonderful life you've been given."

CHAPTER IV

THE TAKE-AWAY ZINGER

★ ★ ★ ★ ★

On October 28, 1980, Governor Reagan engaged in the final debate with President Carter. The election was only a week away. Reagan closed with a rhetorical question. "Are you better off than you were four years ago?" Continuing, he asked:

> *Is our nation stronger and more capable of leading the world toward peace and freedom, or is it weaker? Is there more stability in the world, or less? Are you convinced that we earned the respect of the world and our allies, or has America's position across the globe diminished? Are you personally more secure in your life? Is your family more secure? Is America safer in the world? And most importantly—quite simply—the basic question of our lives: Are you happier today than when Mr. Carter became president of the United States?*

At the time of the debate, the two candidates were relatively close in the polls. After the debate, the Carter percentage began to fall. Reagan's rhetorical question had struck a nerve.

In any major talk, Reagan liked to leave the audience with one ringing or graphic image that would be remembered long after. It might be a catchy aphorism or an arresting word picture that epitomized the thrust of his theme or argument.

British Prime Minister Margaret Thatcher, his political soul mate, was the first head of government to be invited by President Reagan to the White House. She, in turn, reciprocated by delivering an invitation to Reagan to speak to Parliament in 1982. It was unprecedented in British history. Reagan's speech at the Palace of Westminster would be historic and sweeping in its effect in the same way Churchill's Iron Curtain address was in 1946.

Some members of the House of Lords told this author later that the address was the most powerful speech they had ever heard. Reagan said:

> *In an ironic sense, Karl Marx was right. We are witnessing today a great revolutionary crisis, a crisis where the demands of the economic order are conflicting with those of the political order. But the crisis is not happening in the free, non-Marxist world but in the home of Marxism-Leninism—the Soviet Union. It is the Soviet Union that runs against the tide of history by denying human freedom and human dignity.*

Reagan then called for a prophetic plan of action:

> *What I am describing now is a plan and a hope for the long term. The march of freedom and democracy will leave Marxism-Leninism on the* ash heap of history. *[emphasis added]*

Reagan left a graphic image in the audience's mind, just like Churchill had in his Iron Curtain speech in Fulton, Missouri, in 1946:

> *From Stettin in the Baltic to Trieste in the Adriatic, an iron curtain has descended across the continent of Europe.*

A decade earlier, Churchill, in a speech to the House of Commons, described those who wanted to appease Hitler with this analogy:

> *An appeaser is one who feeds the crocodile hoping it will eat him last.*

Or remember President Roosevelt in 1941, when he argued for Lend Lease aid to Britain. During a White House press conference, he offered this analogy in response to a question:

> *Who would not lend his garden hose to a neighbor*
> *whose house is on fire?*

That analogy alone, say some historians, caused the Lend Lease Bill to be enacted by Congress.

Some historians also think that Abraham Lincoln came from behind to win his reelection in 1864 with this homespun comparison of a farmer and his horse.

> *What farmer would change horses in the middle of*
> *crossing a stream?*

Lincoln was the "horse" and the war was the "stream."

Back in the Constitutional Convention, Benjamin Franklin shot down the proposal for a "standing army" with this ribald analogy that delegates went back to their inns chuckling about.

> *A standing army is like an erect member. Although*
> *it may be a source of conjugal bliss and harmony, it often*
> *invokes the urge for foreign adventure.*

"EVIL EMPIRE"

To the National Association of Evangelicals—a convention of two thousand politically moderate Baptists and Methodists—

Reagan's parting zinger was an alliterative phrase of two words. In the centerpiece of his address, he said:

> *So in your discussions of the nuclear freeze proposals, I urge you to be aware of the temptation of pride—the temptation to blithely declare yourselves above it all and label both sides equally at fault, to ignore the facts of history, and the aggressive impulses of an* evil empire, *to simply call the arms race a great misunderstanding and thereby remove yourselves from the struggle between right and wrong. [emphasis added]*

Interestingly, the mainstream media denounced Reagan for such a provocative and simplistic phrase. Years later, Soviet Premier Boris Yeltsen said, "President Reagan was correct. It was an evil empire."

In his thousands of radio broadcasts, Reagan wrote his own copy. He also drafted his remarks when he was the top draw on the speech circuit in the 1950s, after he left his movie career and before he ran for governor of California in 1966.

Franklin Roosevelt was Reagan's early role model in his radio work and later as governor and president. When, as president, a Democrat accused Reagan of destroying the New Deal, he replied:

I was a New Dealer myself and voted four times for Roosevelt as president. I'm trying to destroy LBJ's Great Society, not FDR's New Deal.

ROOSEVELT AND REAGAN

In fact, Reagan remained close to the president's son, Congressman James Roosevelt, who would join him in ferreting out pro-Communists in the Hollywood movie community. James Roosevelt supported Reagan for governor and then for president. He knew of Reagan's deep affection for his father. So did FDR's other sons, Franklin D. Roosevelt, Jr., and John, both of whom respectively voted twice for Reagan as president.

Reagan watched the 1942 movie *Yankee Doodle Dandy* again and again. James Cagney played George M. Cohan, and Captain Jack Young, a jaunty World War I veteran who bore a likeness to FDR, portrayed President Roosevelt.

In one scene, President Roosevelt greets the composer in the Oval Office, and Cagney comes out dancing down the White House stairs afterward. Young, playing Roosevelt, radiated the ebullient and high-spirited enthusiasm of FDR. Reagan said later to aides that that movie was a source of inspiration for him as president. Not that he imitated Roosevelt; he was always Ronald Reagan. But he picked up on FDR's *bonhomie* and jaunty optimism in his presidential role.

In his first years as a sports radio broadcaster in the 1930s, Reagan also noted the deliberate cadences of FDR in the Fireside Chats that became his broadcasting model.

ROOSEVELT, THE KING OF RADIO

A decade before Winston Churchill's wartime speeches of the 1940s, Roosevelt had mastered the radio medium. Franklin Roosevelt had made the radio his own intimate means of talking with the American people.

By listening again and again to Roosevelt's speeches, Reagan came to understand the effects of repetition, rhythm, and strategic pauses that were FDR's secrets in delivery. Reagan, who could pull off a good imitation of Roosevelt's distinctive patrician cadence, had committed to memory the president's talks, savoring some of his most quotable lines.

Along with repetition, Reagan noted Roosevelt's use of alliteration, rhyme, and the arresting metaphor that would etch an unforgettable imprint on the listeners' minds and ears.

RULE OF REPETITION

FDR's most quoted line in his first inaugural address, in 1933, used repetition:

The only thing we have to fear is fear itself.

Almost as much quoted was this line from his second inaugural address, four years later:

I see one-third of the nation ill-housed, ill-clad, and ill-nourished.

Reagan would employ repetitive aphorisms of his own.

Heroes may not be braver than anyone else. They're just braver five minutes longer.

Or:

You can't control the economy without controlling people.

Or:

History is on the side of the free, because freedom is right, and freedom works.

ALLITERATIVE APHORISMS

Roosevelt would use alliteration in describing the difference between the American democracy and fascism.

> *We are free to live and love and laugh, and we face the world with courage and confidence.*

Again in his definition of a party platform, Roosevelt asserted:

> *A party platform is a promissory note to the American electorate that is never paid.*

Reagan would also adopt alliteration in the repetition of the consonant "p" in this aphorism on religion.

> *The Constitution was never meant to prevent people from praying; its declared purpose was to protect their freedom to pray.*

One of Reagan's most quoted lines in his speech to the British Parliament had this alliteration:

> *Regimes planted by bayonets do not take root.*

One of FDR's most pointed uses of rhyme came in his veto of a Congressional bill.

> *This is not a bill for the needy but for the greedy.*

Reagan would coin this rhyming line as a parting zinger about taxes:

> *They have a kind of layaway plan for your lives, which never changes: Americans make; government takes.*

Like Churchill, FDR would sometimes draw from the animal world for a graphic metaphor.

> *No nation can appease the Nazis. No man can tame a tiger into a kitten by stroking it.*

> *Those Americans who believe that we could live under the illusion of isolationism wanted the American eagle to imitate the tactics of an ostrich.*

Reagan, as governor, said this about state taxes:

> *The symbol on our State flag is the Golden Bear. It is not a cow to be milked.*

"RENDEZVOUS WITH DESTINY"

One of the most eloquent addresses in political history was Reagan's "A Time for Choosing," on behalf of Senator Barry Goldwater's presidential candidacy in 1964. It ranks with William Jennings Bryan's "Cross of Gold" speech, which was delivered countless times around the turn of the last century.

Reagan ended his speech with:

> *You and I have a rendezvous with destiny. We'll preserve for our children this last best hope on earth, or we'll sentence them to take the last step in two thousand years of darkness.*

Reagan had lifted the line right from FDR's second inaugural address:

> *This generation has a rendezvous with destiny.*

Reagan honed and polished for each speech a particular gem—but it never sounded forced and oratorical. Reagan relied on a book of synonyms and one of rhyme endings, and he was not ashamed to use them to coin his zinger lines.

Would-be speakers can use the same tools to craft a winning line. Remember, though, you need only one zinger for your talk or presentation. Your audience is unlikely to remember more than one. Do not overuse these techniques, or they will lose their fresh edge.

CHAPTER V

THE REAGAN RECIPE FOR HUMOR

★ ★ ★ ★ ★

General Eisenhower, in his 1952 presidential campaign, may have inspired the greatest slogan for a political button—"I Like Ike." But arguably, the most likeable personality to ever occupy the White House was Ronald Reagan. His left-wing critics may have considered the former actor shallow and stupid, but he never triggered the hate and odium that Nixon and George W. Bush inspired. Even his administration's blunders, such as the Iran-Contra affair, failed to dent his popularity. Colorado Democratic Congresswoman Patricia Schroeder ruefully called him "The Teflon President."

Reagan was manifestly likable. He displayed no smirk like George W. Bush, no scowl like Richard Nixon. Reagan's grin and twinkle in the eye melted even the fiercest of foes.

NO ONE HATES THE HUMOROUS

The prime reason for his likability was his humor. And the secret to that sense of humor was self-deprecation, which was its essence.

Peggy Noonan, his lyric wordsmith, has said of Reagan that he was "a compulsive storyteller." But the stories he most savored telling were those in which he was the butt of the joke. One that Reagan told in the Oval Office to friends and foes was about an English Channel ferry ride from France to England in 1946:

> *I had just finished filming* The Hasty Heart *with Richard Todd and Patricia Neal, and I decided to take a couple weeks of vacation in the Riviera before heading back to the States. With me went the Warner Brothers representative in London, who had an English wife. When it came time to board the Channel ferry back to England, the British wife discovered she had left her passport back in the hotel. So the two of us boarded the ferry without her but with her suitcases, as well as our own.*
>
> *I was the first whose baggage was checked. The lady French customs inspector asked me to open my bags. The first suitcase belonged to the missing English wife.*
>
> *As the inspector went though the lavender-colored bag, she pulled out a pair of frilly panties and lacy bras. She turned to me and said, 'Monsieur, tres jolie!'"*

NEGATIVE NAME DROPPING

The story, which, incidentally, mentioned one of Reagan's best movie roles, would trigger gales of laughter from his listeners, but laughing the loudest would be Reagan himself.

Would-be speakers should ransack their memories for incidents where they came up with egg on their face—particularly if they were with someone famous or at some notable event. This ploy is called "negative name dropping."

I once wrote a speech for a company president who had attended a state dinner at the White House. His wife had bought a new designer gown for the occasion, and he had chosen a new black-tie outfit. Then, in the receiving line, Reagan called him "John" instead of "James," his actual first name. In telling the story, he had let the audience know he was important enough to be invited to the White House. And yet, by telling a story that put him down, he did not seem boastful.

In a speech I once delivered, I mentioned the four-letter Anglo-Saxon words that Henry Kissinger had used in chewing me out for a memo I wrote. By doing so, I shared a humbling anecdote while making it clear that at least Dr. Kissinger had once read my memos.

"THIRD WORLD WAR"

In 1978, Reagan had been selected to speak before the prestigious World Affairs Council in Philadelphia. Reagan was planning to run for president the following year, and he wanted to burnish his foreign policy credentials. In his speech, which I had written, he was supposed to say, "The Third World should be given increased priority"; instead, he said, "The Third World War should be given increased priority." Then, in four other places in the speech where "Third World" was to be said, Reagan inserted a word at the end—"Third World War." At my table, Senators Hugh Scott and Dick Schweiker and former ambassador Walter Annenberg looked at me accusingly. They knew I had drafted the speech.

If you do not have any negative name-dropping experiences, then craft some one-liners that poke fun at yourself.

FOIBLES, FLAWS, AND FEATURES

Most of the witty one-liners Reagan delivered to brighten up his speeches were *bon mots* that poked fun at his foibles and flaws—his age (he had the distinction of being the oldest president to date), his hearing, his forgetfulness, his laziness, or his habit of falling asleep during meetings.

About his advanced age, he remarked on his birthday, February 6, 1982:

Last year, you all helped me begin celebrating the thirty-first anniversary of my thirty-ninth birthday...and I must say, all of those pile up, but an increase of numbers don't bother me at all, because I recall that Moses was eighty when God commissioned him for public service, and he lived to be 120.

He once remarked on his hearing loss:

It's no secret that I wear a hearing aid. Well, just the other day, it went haywire. We discovered the KGB had put a listening device in my listening device.

And about his work habits.

It's true. Hard work never killed anybody, but I figure why take the chance.

The secret for would-be speakers to become more likeable to their audiences is self-deprecating humor. The more likeable they appear when they make their talks or presentations, the more likely their pitches or promotions will find a receptive audience.

Every speaker has at least one obvious flaw or foible or awkward feature—be it too little hair or too much weight.

As a White House speechwriter for Gerald Ford, I wrote some one-liners on behalf of his good friend, sportscaster (and ex-baseball catcher) Joe Garagiola. I had him poke fun at his own baldness.

SHORTNESS, BALDNESS, OR BACKGROUND

Bill Clinton's secretary of labor, Robert Reich, was, at 5'2", perhaps the shortest cabinet secretary since James Madison, who served in Jefferson's cabinet. Reich always began his talks with a funny story about how he once needed a stepladder brought out to the lectern.

On one occasion, a Washington lobbyist asked me to write some one-liners for Democratic Ways and Means Committee Chairman Dan Rostenkowski. (Even though I wrote for only Republican presidents, I would on occasion write humorous one-liners for Democrats, such as George McGovern and Senator "Fritz" Hollings.)

For the crusty Rostenkowski, I crafted one-liners that made fun of his Polish ancestry. "The only thing smarter than a Phi Beta Kappa WASP [Bush] is a dumb Polack." I also took aim at his native Chicago's reputation for corrupt elections: "In my successive victories to Congress, I have established a national record. More dead have voted for me than anyone else in history."

Other obvious fodder included his hapless baseball team, the Chicago Cubs: "I note some of the economists are predicting a bear market. Well, it's not true that the term refers to the Chicago Cubs."

But Rostenkowski refused to use any humor that denigrated his ancestry, city, or baseball team. Instead, he abandoned my lines and wrote his own jokes about Republicans—and bombed.

(As an aside, Rostenkowski did not honor my bill for services. Politicians typically will pony up five thousand dollars for a forty-minute speech, but when they see a page of one-liners, they often balk at paying more than five hundred dollars. They think they pay by the word. But believe me, the highest-paid writers in the country are those who write for Jay Leno [they earn millions]. Crafting witty one-liners is far harder than translating some academic position paper into a talk.)

ONE-LINERS AND NOT JOKES

In adding humor to your own speeches, the first thing to recognize is the difference between the one-liners and the bare-bones joke. A joke, by my definition, is a conversational exchange: "The wife says, 'What would it take for you to go for a second honeymoon?' And the husband replies, 'A second wife.'" The flavor of the one-liner is more like this:

"Let's face it, men. You really need a wife. Think of all the things you can't blame on the government."

A Washington lobbyist once told me, "Humes, I can produce the winning margin in just about any Senate vote if I have ready access to two things—a live-in maid for the Senator's wife and a guy who can do opening one-liners for his speeches back home."

In fact, the ever-rising demand for short, quotable bites is proof that the day of the raconteur is waning. Politicians want to seem more like a wit than a windbag.

Poking fun of his religion, Governor Mitt Romney once said, "I am a Mormon. I firmly believe that marriage is for a man and a woman and a woman and a woman and a woman…" (He also said, when he was surrounded by a cast of his presidential rivals—all of whom were divorced— "Look, I'm the only Mormon here, and yet I'm the only one who's had only one wife.")

A supporter for Obama was asked if she objected to Bill Clinton's presence in his wife's campaign. "No, I've always been attracted to Bill Clinton—I love his face, all two of them."

Would-be speakers would do well to master the structure of the "one-liner," which ironically has two lines, or stages. First comes the "straight line," then the "snapper." In other words, the upbeat beginning is followed by the witty punch line.

STRAIGHT LINE AND SNAPPER

Remember how the master of the one-liner, Bob Hope, would begin his build-up statement with "Seriously folks…" Hope was trying to ensure that his first, upbeat sentence would be perceived as "straight." The more the audience believed his opening line was sincere, the more likely they were to laugh at the snapper. Said Hope in Iraq in 1990, "Seriously, it's great for me to be here in Baghdad—where it's not me who is the one bombing."

Haley Barbour, former Republican national chairman and governor of Mississippi, is another master of self-deprecating podium humor.

> *Thank you for that warm reception, which I so richly deserve…and so seldom get. Seriously, Mr. Chairman, I want to say I truly appreciate your introduction. I especially admire your way with words…the way you don't let yourself be inhibited by the facts. Actually, Mr. Chairman, I have to say that was the second-best introduction I have ever received. The best was a few weeks ago, when the chairman arrived late, and I had to introduce myself.*

Former Secretary of State Alexander Haig—appointed by President Reagan in 1982—spoke to the Ends of the Earth Club in New York City in 2000. Haig had been fired by Reagan after he complained that he was being circumvented by fellow cabinet members Jim Baker and Ed Meese. After I introduced Haig to his audience at the club, he followed with:

> *Thank you, James, for your all-too-generous introduction. It's always nice to be described as a former high public official in government. That sounds better than what I really was—just another bureaucrat without tenure.*
>
> *James was also kind enough not to dwell on some of the details of my sudden departure. But I'll tell you one thing: My brief stint in government was like being a mushroom. They kept me in the dark, they piled on a lot of crap, and then they had me canned.*

Reagan himself, of course, also had a noteworthy technique in crafting one-liners from a straight line followed by a snapper. On his birthday in 1976, Reagan said:

> *Actually, being sixty-five isn't so bad…at my age, being called a sexagenarian sounds like flattery.*

I heard one executive vice president of a brokerage firm say:

I thank the chairman for his introduction, but I don't think he quite spelled out what all that means...That's the title given to a corporate officer instead of a raise.

Really though, I take a lot of satisfaction in being a vice president...It means you can take a two-hour lunch without hindering production.

Seriously though, being a vice president is a real challenge...Not everyone who finds a molehill at nine can make a mountain out of it by five.

A food executive financial officer, who, like this writer, is horizontally challenged, made this comment in the midst of analyzing some statistics: "Let's, for a moment, round out some of those figures...As you can see, I'm an expert in that."

A national firm's marketing executive, whose head was as bald as a cue ball, said,

Actually I take pride in the faith my boss has in me. Last month he said, "Jack, we'll be sending you out to Phoenix. A real hairy situation has developed out there." And I replied, pointing to my dome, "And you're sending me?"

ONE THEME, ONE TOPIC

When you work out some one-liners for yourself, follow

Reagan's rule of sticking to one topic. Do not jump from one to another. Even experienced nightclub comedians cannot pull off the scatter-hit approach.

Some years ago, I was a speaker at a convention in Las Vegas. I attended one of the shows on the strip, and the comedian delivered this set of one-liners on hotel accommodations.

> *I can tell you, I was in one of those very exclusive hotels on the strip…Even the room service had an unlisted number.*
>
> *No really, I can't complain. The management went to great lengths to get me an air-conditioned room…I know— I was there when the bellboy pried open the windows.*
>
> *Yes, they even put Bibles in all the rooms…But by that time, it's too late.*

HIS SECRETS OF WIT

Note the following "straight/snapper" technique exemplified by Reagan in crafting some one-liners about government.

> *A taxpayer is someone who works for the government…but doesn't have to take the secret service exam.*

Some years ago, the federal government declared war on poverty...and poverty won.

But his best humor was directed at himself. Remember, that was the secret to his likability.

My press secretary said the other day that preparing me for a press conference was like reinventing the wheel. It's not true. I was around when the wheel was invented...and it was easier.

And I also remember something Thomas Jefferson once said. He stated: "We should never judge a president by his age, only by his words"...And ever since he told me that, I've stopped worrying.

I heard one presidential candidate [Gary Hart in 1984] say what this country needed was a president for the nineties. I was set to run again...I thought he said a president in his nineties.

His advanced age was Reagan's most frequent vehicle for self-deprecation. But he also touched on other flaws the mainstream media harped on: his supposed simple-mindedness and sluggish work habits.

The greatest of our presidents endear themselves by poking fun at themselves. Abraham Lincoln said once, "My opponent [Stephen Douglas] has accused me of being two-faced. But tell me why, if God gave me two faces, I'd be wearing this one."

Franklin Roosevelt regaled audiences with a tale about a marine gunner at the Battle of Guadalcanal:

> *From his hill position, this Marine machine gunner looked down. All of a sudden, some Japanese infantry charged. Most of them, in their bayonet-thrust advance, were screaming in broken English, "To hell with Roosevelt."*
>
> *The machine gunner sat in his position, stunned. His mate yelled, "Fire! Fire! Why don't you fire?"*
>
> *The gunner answered, "I can't bring myself to shoot a fellow Republican."*

In March 1984, while rumors were rampant that Reagan might run again, Reagan held up a headline from the *Washington Post* and told the press corps:

> *I glanced at this story heralding the return of spring. The headline screams, "THE SAP IS RUNNING AGAIN," and*

I thought they were prematurely releasing my reelection announcement.

Reagan also made this vow to the press corps:

I've laid down the law, though, to everyone. From now on, about any crisis that happens, no matter what time it is, wake me...even if it's in the middle of a cabinet meeting.

Even his most acid critics among the Washington reporters laughed. Regardless of your political leanings, you could not help liking Ronald Reagan.

Remember, in humor, there is one unbeatable element—belittlement of self.

That is the way Reagan turned his flaws and foibles into likability. So you, too, can win success by tossing off one-liners that poke good-natured fun at yourself.

CHAPTER VI

PODIUM PRESENCE

★ ★ ★ ★ ★

Ronald Reagan never wore a Giorgio Armani suit or Yves Saint Laurent jacket in his life. He left the designer labels to his wife. He always looked as if he had picked his suit off the rack in JCPenney or Montgomery Ward. His favorite clothes were like his favorite foods, which were meat and potatoes or macaroni and cheese. Nancy might relish the haute cuisine, but plain and simple was her husband's taste in food, as well as fashion.

"MEAT AND POTATOES" LOOK

But there was more to Reagan's appearance than met the eye, just as there was to his speaking style. Reagan's talks sounded almost conversational and did not reveal the effort behind them. So Reagan's suits were not store-bought, ready to wear. They were actually made by a tailor to fit Reagan's exact specifications in a way that maximized his shoulders and height. He also had his shirts specially crafted for him by a Hollywood tailor to minimize his short neck.

"NO-NECK" RON

Reagan's squat neck almost cost him a Warner Brothers contract in 1936. But then someone with Warner Brothers said, "Jimmy Cagney had the same problem, and we had a shirtmaker design shirts that masked the problem." Behind the neck, the special shirt had the same collar band, but as it encircled the neck, it became narrower and smaller. The tips of the collar laid flat on his chest, revealing a few more inches of skin that would not have been exposed by a normal collar.

In addition, they told the young aspiring actor to stop wearing narrow ties and to use the new Windsor knot, popularized by the recently abdicated British king. A solid-colored tie in a Windsor triangular knot with an extra-wide collar would appear to lengthen his neck. He would wear the same shirts and Windsor-knotted ties ever after in his movie, television, and political careers.

In the White House, swatches of cloth would be brought to the Oval Office, and he would choose the design and material. Advisers like Michael Deaver were often dismayed at Reagan's selections. Reagan preferred brown to dark blue, often with patterns, like checks. Deaver used to say that Reagan's beloved old topcoat, which he refused to replace, was one that even Lieutenant Columbo would have packed off to the Salvation Army.

SHOOT SUIT?

Deaver was aghast at one tailored suit in particular that arrived at the White House. For the suit, Reagan had chosen a swatch of blue-gray pattern, but the pattern screamed when he put it on. He wore it anyway, to the raised eyebrows of both Michael and Nancy. To them it looked like something the *Death of a Salesman* character Willy Loman would have worn.

One day the president asked Deaver, "Mike, what do you really think of this suit?"

"Well," replied Deaver, "to be honest, if you had to be shot, why couldn't you have been wearing this suit?"

NEITHER SAVILE ROW NOR RAZOR HAIRCUTS

There was a "method to his madness" when it came to Reagan's taste. Just as Reagan, from the podium, never preached or pontificated to his listeners, so he did not overdress to impress. As Jean Kirkpatrick told me, "Ronnie never treated himself like a statue of himself." He was one with his audience. He did not wear the Savile Row Co. suits of John Kerry, nor did he sport the four-hundred-dollar razor-cut haircut of John Edwards. Reagan's favorite barber in Santa Barbara did it the old-fashioned way, without gels and a blow-dryer.

FASHION PLATE FAILURES

Too many speakers dress as if they are going to be photographed by *Fortune* magazine. They wear pinstriped suits with British-style white collars on blue shirts. They may also have a kerchief in the top jacket pocket to match their tie, or perhaps a pin under the tie to hold it in place. Jack Kemp was attached to his collar pin. Only with threats to quit did Jack Kemp's advisers succeed in getting Kemp to remove the pin. The day after Jack's defeat for vice president in 1996, he put it back on. Mitt Romney, in his 2008 presidential campaign, dressed like the millionaire CEO he is and talked to audiences as if they were his sales force. His speech, as well as his suit, talked down to them. McCain and Huckabee did not make that mistake. Governor Huckabee told this writer, "Never look like the boss your listeners work for during the day." Huckabee and I were both featured speakers at a Colorado Leadership Conference in April 2008.

SELL IDEAS—UNDERSELL YOURSELF

These executives, by their clothes, advertise their vanity and ambition. Naked ambition turns off audiences. Sell your ideas, but undersell your own importance.

Why do presidential candidates like James Earl Carter, William Jefferson Clinton, Michael Huckabee, or Rudolph

Giuliani change their first names to "Jimmy," "Bill," "Mike," or "Rudy," when they run for higher office? Pretentious is another word for "pompous." It does not make one popular. Reagan refused to take a more glamorous name that his studio thought would appear sexier on a theater marquee. The same way he would not dress up for an audience, he would not change his name. Ron Reagan was what he would be.

Reagan may have dressed like a member of the Rotary Club, but his appearance was almost regal in his close attention to detail. The white shirt was tailor made, just like his suit. His shoes were polished to a shine. He shaved just before every appearance. He was meticulously groomed, but it was not overpowering, like some types of cologne—which, by the way, he never used.

This writer is a communications consultant to a major New York investment firm. I advise them to have solid-colored, tailor-made suits reserved for presentations or speeches and to have made-to-order white shirts (non-button down) with collars and shapes that flatter their faces. But no fancy striped shirts with gaudy cufflinks. Look like the executive you are supposed to be, not a fashion plate.

In 1777, Benjamin Franklin, before the French Court of Louis XVI, wore a plain white American broadcloth with brown deerskin breeches when he pleaded, successfully, the case for a French government loan for the Continental

Congress. He was a simple contrast to the audience of men he faced, all of whom were garbed in satin and velvet.

Franklin's balding head also stood in stark contrast to the powdered wigs of his audience members. When his daughter, Sally, had pressed him to buy more stylish garb before he sailed to France for his appearance before the Court of Versailles, he had told her, "Sally, I want to look more like a pioneer than a prince."

NO TOUPEE FOR THE TOPLESS!

Any speaker with the too-clean lines of a toupee has lost his audience before he opens his mouth. Even worse is the executive who combs over strands of his hair to cover a balding spot. It is worth noting that the last president who had a beard, William Howard Taft, was beaten for reelection in 1912. And the only presidential candidate who sported a moustache was New York Governor Thomas Dewey, who, though heavily favored to win, lost to President Truman in 1948. Theodore Roosevelt's daughter, Alice Longworth, said, "Dewey looked like the little man on the wedding cake."

In 1936, when Reagan signed up for a movie contract, the studio not only wanted to change his name to something more glamorous but wanted to change his appearance by adding a moustache to look more like the male matinee idols of the day—Robert Taylor,

Clark Gable, and William Powell. Reagan refused. To Reagan, moustaches were more vanity than virility. He would remain Ron Reagan without any moustache.

As a speaker, do not get caught in any potentially embarrassing acts of vanity, like, for instance, wearing two-inch lifts in your heels. A candidate for governor recently was caught with lifts by a photographer who compared the candidate's height in two different photographs where he was standing next to the same politician. It may sound silly, but his campaign faltered, never to rise again.

Incidentally, this gubernatorial candidate's hero was Ronald Reagan, so maybe he had heard the story of how Reagan had once cheated to make himself look taller.

In 1939, Reagan was doing promotional shots with co-star Errol Flynn for their picture *Santa Fe Trail*. Both were going to be photographed in cowboy regalia with pistols at the ready. Reagan knew he was a better horseman than Flynn, but he also knew he was two inches shorter. And Reagan wanted to get the lead in future cowboy films.

So while they waited for the photographer, Reagan engaged Flynn in talking while subtly kicking up the desert turf. When the cameraman came, Reagan had two inches of dirt to stand on, making him appear as tall as Flynn. Reagan loved regaling the story to others (including Flynn) later.

The difference is that Reagan operated in make-believe

Hollywood and not in the "gotcha" reality of present-day politics. And contrary to President Gerry Ford's jibe in 1976, "Reagan doesn't dye his hair, it's just prematurely orange," Reagan did not dye his hair. It remained brown to his death.

LANKY LINCOLN

Make your flaws in face, figure, and size work for you. An Episcopal priest friend of mine shaved his balding head to look like a dome. It enhanced his pulpit authority.

Abraham Lincoln made his 6'4" gawkiness an asset by wearing a stovepipe hat and long shawl that went down past his waist to maximize his height. He wanted to make a caricature of himself that would endear him to audiences.

Female readers do not have to be reminded that looking sexy is not necessarily dressing for success. You are not Dolly Parton or Paris Hilton. In the business world, fashion disasters are those that show too much cleavage and too little coverage—too much leg and too little common sense.

The advice applies to your scent, as well as your suit. Women who reek like the makeup assistant at Bloomingdales do not make it in the corporate world.

ACCESSORIES TO ACCENTUATE

Remember, simplicity in style works best. Keep your suits solid in color. Let the accessories—such as a delicate gold chain, pearl necklace, or silk scarf—frame your suit or dress. Remember, busy designs can make you appear not only fatter but older.

One day in 1986, after a picture in the paper showed Reagan riding a horse at his ranch in Santa Barbara, an old Hollywood friend called and said, "How come you look younger every time I see you?"

"I ride older horses," he replied.

When you choose older, simpler, traditional styles, instead of flashy new ones, you will look younger.

CHAPTER VII

VOICE IS VERSE

★ ★ ★ ★ ★

Whered World War II ended, Reagan found that his acting career was slow to resume. At the same time, Reagan, who had always been active in the Screen Actors Guild, took alarming notice of the rising Communist party's influence in this Hollywood union. One who agreed with him was Jimmy Roosevelt. Jimmy's father, FDR, had always been Reagan's role model.

As Reagan's acting career dissolved, his demand as a speaker and his role as a Screen Actors Guild representative served as a replacement. His warnings about Communist infiltration then triggered anonymous threats. Reagan was advised to carry a gun. Jimmy Roosevelt, who had been the principal speaker against the Red influence in Hollywood, would win a Congressional seat in 1948 and then would refer to his friend, Ronald Reagan, any speech requests in California he could not accept because of his duties in Washington.

In his developing friendship with Jimmy Roosevelt, Reagan asked him to tell him more about his father's speaking techniques and Winston Churchill's oratorical secrets as well. Jimmy Roosevelt had been there in December 1941 when Prime Minister Churchill visited Washington and delivered an address to a joint session of Congress.

ENDING A LINE WITH THE'S AND OF'S

In one White House anecdote that Jimmy shared with Reagan, Churchill was in the Monroe Room preparing his draft. He barked at a temporary secretary, "Who's been ending my lines with 'the's' and 'of's'?" It was Churchill's obsession that a speech should not sound like an article read aloud, and neither should it be written that way. So he was very particular about the way his speeches were typed.

Jimmy had seen firsthand a copy of the Churchill address to Congress in December 1941 that had been sent to the White House. It was not in the usual article form, which typically looks like most of this page, with each line ending in the right margin when space runs out.

Churchill had shared with President Roosevelt this trick because both were fascinated by the structuring and shaping of speeches. Both were also masters of the radio medium. Actually, FDR was a bit put out when he learned that the British Prime Minister never employed the assistance of a speechwriter. By contrast, Roosevelt had two former Pulitzer Prize winners on his payroll—Robert Sherwood, author of *Abe Lincoln in Illinois*, and the poet Archibald MacLeish. Roosevelt agreed with Churchill when the Prime Minister told him, "Every speech is a rhymeless, meterless verse."

WRITTEN FOR THE EAR, NOT THE EYE

And so continued Churchill, "It should be written out like verse, because it is written for the ear, not the eye."

Note the way Churchill had his Joint Session of Congress speech typed.

> *After the outrages*
> *they have committed on us*
> *at Pearl Harbor*
> *in the Pacific Islands*
> *in Malaya*
> *and the Dutch East Indies*
> *it becomes difficult*
> *to reconcile Japanese action*
> *with prudence or sanity.*
> *What kind of people*
> *do they think we are?*

The audience erupted with five minutes of a standing, tumultuous applause—the longest standing ovation in Congressional history.

And observe the way Churchill spaced out the ending of the speech he delivered to Congress.

> *It is not given to us to peer*
> *into the mysteries of the future.*
> *Still I avow my hope and faith*
> *sure and inviolate*
> *that in the days to come*
> *the British and American people*
> *will for their own safety*
> *and for their good of all*
> *walk together*
> *in majesty*
> *in justice*
> *and in peace.*

Upon hearing this story from the young Roosevelt, Reagan realized he had employed a similar technique while writing scripts for his radio commentary in the early 1930s. Now he adopted Churchill's method in typing out his talks on Communist infiltration in Hollywood.

In preparing each address, he would speak aloud and then type his words in a series of lines like verse. That would help him to craft a talk, not an article. "No article that is read out," Reagan would say, "is really a speech."

LISTENING MACHINES TURNED UP FULL?

In his years on the speech circuit, Reagan came to know that just because his own "talking machine" was turned up full did not mean that those in the audience had their "listening machines" turned up, too.

Think back to how many times you have delivered a talk and afterward had someone ask you, "Why didn't you mention packaging or quality control?" when the answer is that you did—but apparently it had not registered.

NO TUBE FROM SPEAKER'S MOUTH TO LISTENER'S EAR

When you read an article, your eye falls on every word. But do not assume that when you are speaking, every word you utter registers in every listener's ear. There is no tube from the lectern that carries the speaker's words to the listeners' ears. That is why you can effectively pack more statistics and facts into an article than you can in a talk.

An article is more like a photograph, a realistic and accurate portrayal of physical features, but a speech is more like a political caricature. It is an artistic exaggeration that is a powerful projection of a point of view.

REPETITION NOT A VICE BUT A DEVICE

When Reagan began drafting his own remarks, he recognized

one big difference between an article and a speech. He remembered that at Eureka College his book reports garnered the same comment from his instructors in the margin: "Redundant." In speaking, however, Reagan discovered that repetition is not a vice but a device. Like a refrain in a song, it is a poetic ploy for the ear. Yet, it is also an enhancement and enforcement of the message.

In his concession speech in Kansas City at the Republican National Convention in 1976, Reagan said to his delegates:

> *Don't get cynical.*
> *Don't get cynical,*
> *because look at yourselves*
> *and what you were willing to do*
> *and recognize that there are*
> *millions and millions of Americans out there*
> *that want what you want*
> *that want it to be that way*
> *that want it to be*
> *a shining city on the hill.*

Whenever he typed a talk as a text to read from, Reagan had three rules for clustering words on a line.

After every period or comma, end the line.

Do not separate the preposition from its object.

And like Churchill, never end a line with "the" or "of."

Remember, if you space out your speech text like Reagan, you will sound and succeed like Reagan.

CHAPTER VIII

READ A SPEECH LIKE REAGAN

★ ★ ★ ★ ★

In 1946, Reagan went to Britain to resume his acting career after his wartime service. He played the supporting
role as "Yank" to British actor Richard Todd in the film
version of the play *The Hasty Heart*. Post-war London was
bleak under the British Labourite government, and Democratic Reagan found himself supporting opposition leader
Winston Churchill in his attacks on socialism. He would
go to the Strangers Gallery in the House of Commons to
listen to Churchill. Reagan also attended the former Prime
Minister's speech when he delivered a talk to the Royal
Academy of Arts.

CHURCHILL TECHNIQUE

Afterward, Reagan saw the text of the speech reported in
the newspaper. It was printed out like an article or essay. He
knew, though, that during the live version it had appeared
to the audience as if the Prime Minister was speaking from
only notes. Churchill never uttered phrases or sentences
while looking down, and he always looked at his audience
as he delivered his words.

Reagan had viewed Roosevelt as a model, but now he wanted to find out more about Churchill's technique.

Reagan was delighted to discover that Churchill used a similar technique that Reagan had worked out for himself while reading advertisements for radio copy.

REAGAN CANNED FROM FIRST RADIO JOB

Reagan was actually fired from his first radio job. He had answered an ad for a position with a radio station in Des Moines, Iowa, after graduating from Eureka. His resonant baritone and college acting experience had landed him the job.

Over the air, Reagan projected a warm personality with an easy flow of upbeat conversation, but he flopped when he read the commercials for department stores and car dealers and the other local radio advertisers. The vivacity left his voice. His phrasing was stilted and flat.

He found the solution by listening to Roosevelt's Fireside Chats. Reagan knew FDR was reading from his text, but he sounded conversational, relaxed, and believable.

FDR IN NEWS FILMS

Reagan practiced his radio technique by reading FDR's speeches. He watched Roosevelt in Movietone News clips before films, and he discovered that FDR seemed to be looking down at a phrase or short sentence and then uttering it while looking at the audience. He knew he could simulate Roosevelt's easy, flowing style. The technique was not new to Reagan. In college, he had used this technique while auditioning for roles in plays. He often had been picked for the best roles because he looked at the play director while reading his lines, while the other aspiring actors did not.

When the broadcaster who had taken over Reagan's radio job left for a bigger station, Reagan got another chance. This time, when reading the ads, he would look at the copy and memorize a phrase or two. "Freedom Buick is offering a great deal." Then he would cover the ad with his hand, look up, and conversationally say the memorized line into the microphone.

Reagan would then look down at the copy again and put to memory the next line. "Why, for only one hundred dollars, you can drive away in a brand-new Buick."

The new technique made him popular with Iowan radio advertisers. Reagan had discovered the secret perfected by the two greatest masters of radio communication in the twentieth century—Franklin Roosevelt and Winston Churchill.

FRED FIZZLES

In the 2008 presidential campaign, many political conservatives first looked to Fred Thompson as the one who might possess a lot of Reagan's communication skills. After all, he had successfully acted on television. Yet, in his first speech after his presidential announcement, Thompson flopped. It was an address to a national conference of Republican state legislators. He read the speech aloud while looking down and not at his audience. The result was dull, flat, and uninspiring. The appearance that was supposed to ignite the campaign failed to provide the spark.

Over the years, I have heard even renowned speakers like Lee Iacocca and Jack Kemp disappoint audiences who had expected to be swept off their feet. Both are outstanding when they speak without a text, but they have not yet figured out how to read a speech effectively.

Often, when I am engaged to draft a speech for a company executive, the CEO will tell me, "Humes, I don't like the speeches written out. I'm more comfortable with a few notes in front of me and then to speak from them." I tell him the maxim: Bad speakers read speeches. Good speakers read from notes. Great speakers read their speeches. Memorable lines do not emerge talking extemporaneously from a few notes.

Reagan's "Marxism on the ashes of history" and "evil empire" were the result of assiduously crafted addresses. Kennedy did not ad-lib "Ask not what your country can do for you," nor was Martin Luther King Jr's "I have a dream" oration extemporaneous.

If you want your talk to be memorable, draft it out first. Then you can reduce it to notes if you must. But better to master the technique of reading a speech like Reagan.

Lee Bowman (who once played Ellery Queen in the early days of television) was an actor friend of Reagan. When Bowman's acting days were over, he headed a company in communication consulting. He would travel across the country advising CEOs on how to read a text without looking as if they were reading by using Reagan's technique. When Bowman suddenly died, his son, Lee Bowman, Jr., made me president of the company.

DYNAMO OR DRONE?

Following the practice of the senior Bowman, we made it a rule to videotape each executive client when he or she was talking informally about the company and the principal problems facing the industry. Then we videotaped the client reading a well-written speech by a current business executive. The comparison was dramatic. When he was conversational, he was dynamic—when he read, he droned.

Even when each executive tried to put more force in his or her delivery, the result was more artificial than authoritative. The client was speaking at us—not to us. The pace of delivery was too rapid and the rhythm too unvaried to seem like the natural flow of conversation.

DO NOT PHOTOGRAPH TOO LONG A PHRASE

"Photograph a phrase in your eye," advised Reagan. "Then look up and deliver the phrase."

Try this Reagan closer at the Palace of Westminster in London in 1982.

> *Let us now begin*
> *a major effort to secure the best;*
> *a crusade for freedom*
> *that will engage the faith and fortitude*
> *of the next generation.*

Do not try to read the words—rather, try to record a picture of each phrase with your eye. In doing so, do not attempt to eye-photograph a whole sentence or too long a phrase.

Let your eye record only what it can comfortably commit to memory. If you forget the last part after you have raised your head, don't sweat it. Look down and fix the unremembered part in your mind, and then repeat the entire phrase. In fact, it will sound more conversational if you do have to repeat yourself. Most of us in conversation repeat phrases while talking.

FORGET A BIT? DON'T SWEAT IT

Great speakers like Franklin Roosevelt, Winston Churchill, and Ronald Reagan read their speeches. They know how to read a speech while maintaining eye contact with their audience.

Every time you look down and read a line, you cut off the current and flow you've established with your audience. It is like stepping on a power cord meant to convey your message and yanking it from its plug.

Pick up a *Wall Street Journal* editorial and try this exercise in reading.

Look down and eye-photograph.

Look up and pause.

Deliver the phrase and pause.

Look down and eye-photograph another "snatch" of words. (That is what Churchill called it.)

Look up and pause.

Deliver another phrase and pause.

PAUSE IS PARAMOUNT

Remember, the pause is the major tool in reading the talk. It not only helps you to eye-photograph phrase by phrase, but even more important, it also helps the audience to digest your words more easily. The lack of pauses is one of the reasons speeches that are obviously read sound unnatural and strain the listener's ears. The speech has too rapid a pace, so it does not sound conversational but artificial.

CEOs who I rehearse in delivering a talk often feel uncomfortable with the pause—they think it is too long. They think that in one or two seconds they are going to lose their audience. Invariably, they start to deliver the phrase they just eye-photographed as soon as their eyes rise from the page below them. That is a no-no! You have to pause before you voice the phrase you have just etched in your mind. It is the pause that makes the audience believe that you are not reading the speech but only looking down at notes.

PAUSE IS A PLOY

Have you ever run out of gas and poured gas from a can back into the tank? You will remember how the narrow tube often rejects and triggers a backflow or overflow. In the same way, listeners reject a speech that is merely read to them. Not only does it sound boring without a pause, but an overfilled ear will turn off and not digest the words.

The pause may seem an eternity to you, but to your audience, it is a microsecond that "punctuates" the sentence, builds anticipation, and aids in the listener's understanding.

Does the pause still sound labored and stilted? Does it sound artificially jarring and jerky? Maybe it does to you, but to your audience, you will sound like Ronald Reagan.

SEE, STOP, SAY

Remember the Reagan recipe for speaking—see, stop, say. Look down and see the text. Look up, all the way up, and stop. Then say the phrase you have recorded in your mind.

In coaching CEOs, I find that in the beginning they remember to pause after looking up from their text, but in a little while, they slide back into voicing their delivery just as they are in the process of lifting their eyes from the page. Always pause a microsecond before speaking out that next phrase you have just committed to memory.

You can catch the knack of speaking this way by watching others. You will better understand after listening to politicians, preachers, or company presidents how most of them fail to maintain eye contact with their audience or control their pace of delivery.

The pause, then, is the major tool in reading a speech, not only for memorizing the phrases to deliver but also for allowing the listeners to absorb them.

Remember, if you want to win over audiences like Reagan, then read a talk like Reagan.

CHAPTER IX

EAT, DRINK, AND BE SORRY

★ ★ ★ ★ ★

Alcohol loosens the tongue," the adage goes. Some hosts would say that to Reagan as they offered him a tray of drinks at a reception when he would be the featured speaker. Reagan on one occasion replied, "No thanks. I remember that warning back in World War II. 'Loose lips sink ships,' and they can sink speakers, too!"

To friends visiting the White House, Reagan would tell the story of a nationally known business executive, Peter Grace, who served on a White House Commission making recommendations on the family. Grace—a lay leader in the Catholic church—once delivered a feature address after imbibing one too many glasses of wine at a reception.

"To feces and the right to life," the executive thundered, using the wrong word for "fetus." "You were first a feces. I was first a feces." Then Grace continued, "We were all feces." Reagan whispered to his neighbor at the head table, "That's when the feces hit the fan."

LOOSE LIPS SINK SHIPS— AND SPEAKERS, TOO

As a student of American history, Reagan knew about the experience of Andrew Johnson, who was so nervous about giving his inaugural address as vice president in 1865 that he took more than a few belts from a pocket flask of bourbon. The result was that he floundered in his speech and eventually collapsed, unable to complete it.

There is a certain kind of relaxant medicine that physicians prescribe for stage fright, but it is not alcohol. At the thousands of dinners where Reagan was the visiting speaker, he was never known even to sip a glass of wine at the reception or at the dinner. At state dinners, where wine is always served, a glass would be seen in front of him. But he took only an obligatory sip in case of a toast to a head of state. He wanted to keep his head clear for remarks.

CONCENTRATION, NOT RELAXATION

In 1952, Reagan played Hall of Famer pitcher Grover Cleveland "Old Pete" Alexander in the movie *The Winning Team*. Rumors had circulated in Alexander's baseball days that "Old Pete" was a drunk. Reagan was told by Alexander's family that it was a disease akin to epilepsy, but its symptoms suggested drunkenness. Anyway, Reagan compared speaking at the podium to pitching on the mound. "It's total concentration, if you don't read from a text or only glance briefly at notes. You have to have total concentration like a pitcher towards a batter. You must have thoroughly prepared your talk, and you don't want to forget anything. I know that if I had even one glass of wine, I'd blame any lapse on that one drink." Reagan did not want to appear sluggish at the podium. For that reason, he also never touched his food at the head table. He did not want to lose his edge or sharpness.

Reagan, who could mimic Churchill, relished telling the familiar anecdote of Churchill colliding with a fat, ugly lady. The woman was Bessie Braddock, a Labourite, who was all of five-foot-two and two hundred pounds. As the two circled in different directions to record their votes, "a division," Churchill, who had been imbibing at the Member's Bar, collided with Braddock.

Braddock said, "Winston, you are drunk, and what's more, disgracefully drunk." And Churchill replied, "Bessie, you are ugly, and what's more, disgracefully ugly. But tomorrow I shall be sober."

Churchill actually did no heavy drinking before speaking, and anyway there is only one Churchill in history. Food can be almost as bad as booze. Those banquet meals of soup, salad, beef, vegetables, and dessert, not to mention a roll with butter, would render anyone stagnant and sluggish.

OVEREAT AND UNDER-SPEAK

Did you ever watch a wildlife program with clips showing a lion after he feasted on a zebra, or a python after he swallowed a wild boar? They are fast asleep.

One circus anecdote that Reagan told was about a lion that did not eat a lamb that was lying next to him. Reagan told it to indicate the naïveté and credulousness of his predecessor, Jimmy Carter, in dealing with dictators. President Carter once kissed Soviet Premier Leonid Brezhnev and invited the North Korean dictator, Kim Il Sung, to talk to a Sunday school class. Carter even accepted a boatload of criminals from Castro.

LION AND THE LAMB

To mock Carter's inclination to appease despots to further the cause of peace, Reagan told the story of the circus impresario in Berlin.

> *This promoter put on a unique show that featured a lion placidly sitting next to a lamb. Above it, he proclaimed the words from Isaiah, "and the lion shall lie down with the lamb."*
>
> *One impressed viewer had a business friend who knew the promoter, and he arranged an introduction. "Tell me, how did you pull off this act. I mean, is it the lion you picked?"*

"No," the promoter replied. "You could do it with any lion. All you have to do is feed him two lambs before you send him on stage with the third."

On one occasion, after Reagan left office, I sat with him in a backroom, behind the head table, just before he was to make a speech to a national business trade association.

Before him was a pot of hot water and a big chocolate chip cookie wrapped in aluminum foil. "This is my speech meal." He said, "I learned this from a preacher friend and a crooner pal." I learned later it was Dr. Billy Graham and Frank Sinatra.

HOT WATER AND A CHOCOLATE CHIP COOKIE

It was a pot of hot water, not tea. Tea (and coffee even more so) possesses caffeine, and caffeine has a clotting or drying affect on the mouth. This writer, who has delivered talks in all fifty states, used to always refuse drink or food before speaking. (But I might treat myself to a martini or two, along with a big sandwich, after the talk.) During the reception, I would take a glass of Diet Coke with lemon, and during dinner, only iced tea. After this advice from Reagan, I abandoned the Diet Coke in favor of orange juice.

Mind you, Reagan sipped his cup of hot water before the talk, not the glass of ice water during the talk that is always put on the podium for the speaker's benefit.

Graham and Sinatra guarded their vocal chords zealously. It was the organ of their profession, and they tended to it like a concert pianist would his Steinway or a violinist his Stradivarius.

Hot water—not cold—soothes and preserves aging vocal chords. The chocolate chip cookie gives a quick sugar burst of energy for speech delivery. As Reagan unwrapped the aluminum foil from the big cookie, he shared with me another tip. "I put on a fresh pair of shoes before I make a speech. The new spring in my step recharges my batteries."

NO BUTTER, NO ICE CREAM

The great communicator added some more advice about eating.

"Now if you're at the head table and have to eat something, whatever you do, don't put any dairy product in your mouth. Butter, creamy salad dressing, ice cream, all will clot up your mouth."

NO DRINK, NO DINNER, NO DAIRY

So if you have to give a presentation, remember Reagan's 3 D's—no drink, no dinner, no dairy.

CHAPTER X

NO POWERPOINTS, GRAPHS, OR SLIDES

★ ★ ★ ★ ★

President Reagan was once showing visitors the Cabinet Room. He pointed to the chair at the head of the cabinet table and remarked, "Some day they will have a sign here saying, 'President Reagan slept here.'"

SLEEPY SLIDES?

True, Reagan did occasionally doze off during some presentations made to him. Most likely it was somebody from the Pentagon delivering a PowerPoint presentation, complete with charts, graphs, or slides.

In his thousands of speeches across the country, Reagan never delivered a PowerPoint talk. Nor did he employ slides and graphs to sell his policies. In promoting his tax cuts in 1982, he let the Secretary of Treasury supply the graphs on the revenue increase the tax cuts would yield. Instead, Reagan talked about growing jobs and growing the economy with personal stories and anecdotes to support his theme.

One of my CEO clients heads a company that employs a full-sized department with the sole purpose of crafting state-of-the-art slides and charts. The CEO told me, "Humes, you know the Chinese maxim: 'One picture is worth a thousand words.'" To which I replied, "I like better the one that states: 'The tongue can paint what the eye can't see.'"

EXECUTIVE, NOT ENGINEER

Reagan was no fan of the practice of bringing in slides for a talk. To Reagan, it reflected the style of an engineer, not an executive. When you speak from the podium, you are in a leadership role. Reagan figured that one demoted himself to a mere technician when he took a backseat to slides.

For many company presidents, the slides become a crutch—forensically the cane or staff for a speech cripple to lean on. When slides are featured, the audience's eyes are focused on the pictures, not on the speaker himself.

Top salesmen—be they insurance agents from the "million-dollar roundtable" or "Avon Ladies" calling on neighbors—will tell you, as Reagan once told a Cabinet secretary advancing his programs, "You have to sell yourself first. If you do that, the program almost sells itself."

CAPTAIN OR CLERK?

When the speaker or salesperson shifts the burden of persuasion to slides or samples, he or she comes off not as a dynamic authority but as a drab nerd who runs the projector and flips through the exhibits.

Reagan's greatest political friend was the fellow head of government "across the pond," Margaret Thatcher. The two shared a disdain for the wimpish behavior of robotic cabinet types who hid behind graphs and charts. One evening, after an extended cabinet meeting where many slides, statistics, and charts were brandished, Thatcher adjourned the meeting and said that she would take everyone present to dinner at a nearby bistro. At the restaurant, the waiter began to describe the specials. Thatcher cut him off tersely: "I'll have the pasta." Then the waiter asked, "And the veggies?" Thatcher answered, "They'll have the pasta too!"

BE MORE THAN YOUR VISUALS

By relying on slides and charts, many top executives make the mistake of demeaning themselves by deferring to visual aids. Why? One could say that Americans, particularly in the business world, have a naïve faith in anything mechanical.

MECHANICAL MANIA

A lot of males are suckers for any new mechanical toy. Show them a new gadget or gizmo, and their eyes light up. But there is a more basic reason executives hide behind technology: fear—the fear of getting up before an audience to speak. A *Reader's Digest* article once said that in the list of fears, standing up in front of an audience ranks first, cancer second, and death third! When I called on a company as a communications consultant, the company president told me, "Humes, look, I'm no Reagan. I'm no governor or congressman. I'm not on any ego trip, and I don't care if I come off as a big shot. I just want to get the facts across, and the best way to do that is with these slides and graphs." And then he unfailingly added, "You know a picture is proof." But Reagan would have countered by saying that a series of pictures is no substitute for the personal beliefs and experiences of the speaker himself.

Reagan, as I said earlier, in his speeches on the circuit or his political campaign, never used a slide presentation. Mitt Romney, in his try for the GOP nomination in 2008, made a practice of it and failed. A PowerPoint is a series of dry facts mounting to an inescapable conclusion—sometimes supported by slides and graphs. Facts are featured, but the presenter may fail to sell himself, just as Romney failed to sell himself to his audience on the campaign trail. During the same primary, whatever fault one found in Governor Huckabee's policies, it's difficult to deny he did sell his engaging and infectious personality and connect with his listeners.

THE "LIKEABLE" LEADER

Most of the time, in presidential campaigns, the more "likeable" candidate wins, e.g., Reagan over Carter in 1980, Bush (41) over Dukakis in 1988, Clinton over Bush (41) in 1992, Clinton over Dole in 1996, Bush (43) over Gore in 2000, and Bush (43) over Kerry in 2004. Romney, with square-jawed, handsome, chiseled features, looked like he came from Central Casting to play the role of president, but the audiences never quite warmed up to this photogenic candidate and his wife and family.

If he had been running for CEO of my company, the Massachusetts governor would have had my vote. He had turned around a bankrupt Olympic program in Utah and then turned around a bankrupt state. But as a future CEO of the country, he did not quite connect. He gave, in a sense, PowerPoint types of presentations on what he had done in the Olympic program and in Massachusetts and then on what he was going to do as president to grow more jobs in the country. Huckabee, though arguably less qualified on paper, was more anecdotal and more likeable.

For a candidate to be more likeable, he or she has to share with audiences pieces of him- or herself—personal experiences, like Reagan did.

EMOTIONAL PIECE OF SELF

I once wrote a speech for Pete Dawkins, who was running for Senator of New Jersey. Dawkins was a former All-American athlete, Heisman Trophy winner, Rhodes Scholar, and Vietnam War general who ended up as a CEO of a major corporation. On the podium, he looked like a blond version of a Greek god. His opponent was Frank Lautenberg, a balding, shortish, middle-aged businessman.

Dawkins invited me to breakfast in the Mayflower Hotel in Washington to ask me about writing some speeches for him. At the end of the breakfast, I asked him for one poignant story from his life. He said he could not think of any. I asked him to think—again— perhaps a shared experience with a grandfather who had died, some words of wisdom a favorite teacher had told him, or, conversely, even something he had failed at, but learned from. Dawkins shook his head. "Well," I replied, "I can remember when you dropped the opening kickoff in the Army–Navy game."

Dawkins replied, "I can't talk about that." Of course, his reluctance to talk was not the reason he lost, but it was symptomatic of the way he came off with his Power-Point presentations. He missed valuable opportunities to win his audience's affection by sharing a piece of himself. He could have talked about the lesson he learned on the football field that afternoon in Philadelphia, which was that one always has to keep his eye on the ball. In talking about his historic fumble, the revelation by this perfect-looking specimen would have endeared him to his audiences.

Several years ago at a meeting at the Union Club in New York City, I heard a talk on World War I. The speaker had written a fascinating book based on oral reminiscences of veterans of that war. Since I was to introduce him, I had not only read the book but made a point of engaging him in conversation at the head table. He proved to make our conversation as interesting as his writing.

INTRODUCTION TO SLIDES

Yet, the speech that followed was not a talk but a series of introductions to slides. "Here is a picture of a tank used at the Battle of the Somme...And here is a picture of General Pershing..." The book had revealed that "Black Jack" Pershing was far more vivid and memorable than his one-dimensional stiff photograph showed. The speaker had made the mistake of subordinating himself to the slide projector, and his speech was comprised of little more than verbal captions for a disjointed series of pictures.

The problem with slides is just that: It is easier to think of some introductory comments to each slide than to prepare a proper presentation with slides employed only for occasional dramatic reinforcement. A visual display should not be a security blanket to hide behind, but rather a handkerchief to pull out of the sleeve. Otherwise, the speaker comes off as second-best, and the slides are shown to their worst advantage.

PAINTING A PICTURE

Some years ago, a travel agent I knew was trying to promote a Bermuda package tour to a director of a trade association. When she arrived at her hotel room, she looked in her briefcase and discovered she had forgotten the photographs of the beach and the resort. Nevertheless, she did not cancel the appointment but worked up notes in her hotel room about what she had experienced when she had stayed in Bermuda a few years before.

To the association director, she waxed poetic about an old pirate's cove she and her husband visited on a second honeymoon. "We rented a boat and rowed across the lagoon in the glow of an island sunset," she told him. She painted a story of romantic rides with picnic lunches prepared by the hotel. She exulted about Bermuda being the combination of a quaint English village with an island beach. And, well, she won the sale, even though no one from her agency had ever managed to sell that particular trade association a package travel deal before.

She later told me, "It was a great step in career development—not that I didn't need the picture packet, but I learned the real secret of selling—that a personal story sells better than an impersonal slide."

Ronald Reagan was a master salesman. Instead of slides, he told stories. He knew from his years on radio that one could create for the ear images that would last longer than those created for the eye on television.

Cabinet secretaries, agency directors, and White House staff members all knew that if you wanted to sell Reagan on a program, you should draft a short talk that the president might use later in promoting it.

Similarly, Reagan's aides would advise those planning to make presentations to Reagan to be aware of his bias against visual aids. "Don't use too many, and if you do, here are his rules," they'd tell you. Some framed them as "Reagan's Ten Commandments."

TEN COMMANDMENTS OF VISUAL AIDS

Thou shalt not use displays that are not bold and arresting in appeal.

Thou shalt not have captions accompanying the slides with more than one line.

Thou shalt not overburden the caption with "corporatese" jargon.

Thou shalt not make the printed text too small.

Thou shalt not keep a detracting pointer or directing stick in your hand throughout the presentation.

Thou shalt not leave a slide in view when you have finished discussing it.

Thou shalt not make the whole presentation in a darkened room that induces sleep.

Thou shalt not use linear graphs; instead, opt for bar graphs with different colors.

Thou shalt not read your speech off slides.

Thou shalt not deliver a series of commentaries on a series of exhibits or slides.

CHAPTER XI

"CASE THE JOINT"

★ ★ ★ ★ ★

In 1979, I went to Newport, Rhode Island, to perform my one-man Churchill show. With me in Newport was Olivia de Havilland. We had flown up together in a private plane from New York. Her talk was called "Gone with the Wind," which referred to the film (she, who had played Melanie Hamilton, was the last surviving member of the cast) and to the old days of the "big studio" movies. She introduced me the first night, and I presented her the second night. I include my introduction here because she told me, "You introduce me in the way Ronnie would have."

Marion Morrison, Archibald Leach, and Norma Jeane Mortenson—only their respective fans know they are the birth names of John Wayne, Cary Grant, and Marilyn Monroe. Our artist's name is the one she was christened with—Olivia. Her father was an Anglican rector on the Isle of Jersey off the coast of France, and he chose the name of his favorite character in Shakespeare's Twelfth Night.

The name Havilland was the name of the Havilland airplane motors in World War II. Her uncle, Sir

Geoffrey, headed the family firm. But her French cousin, Reneé Havilland, manufactured the porcelain china of that name.

In her Academy Award-winning movie The Heiress *in 1949, as well as* The Snake Pit *the year before, Olivia manifested all the tensile power of those engines that won the Battle of Britain in 1940, and all the delicate beauty of the exquisite china that graces so many tables.*

I struck up a friendship with the actress legend, and she gave me some pointers on speaking. Olivia had continued in major acting roles long after Reagan left his movie career. But when she, in her later years, started to go out on the speech circuit, she asked her friend Ronnie for advice. (They had once acted together in *Santa Fe Trail* in 1940.) Later, after the war, she would join Jimmy Roosevelt (the late Franklin Roosevelt's son) and Reagan in ferreting out the pro-Communist directors and writers in Hollywood. She said to me, "Even if Ronnie never won an Academy Award as an actor, he should have won a special Oscar for his heroic role in battling the Communist influence in Hollywood."

"FIRST, CASE THE JOINT"

Olivia said, "Jamie, when I began the speech circuit, Ronnie told me in a mock gangster voice, 'First, Olivia, you have to case the joint.'" Together, Olivia and I went to the stage of the theater where we were to speak. She stood in different places in the theater to check how my voice was coming across.

We were both doing one-person shows. She drew a chalk X on the spot where we would be standing and then paced off how many steps we should take to the left or right.

When Reagan became governor of California, his staff did the work of advancing each speech and checking out every speech forum. At the White House, Mick Denver was the "super maestro" in charge of "atmospherics," as he called it. But when he was a number one on the dinner circuit, Reagan would arrive early and "case the joint" himself.

One time he learned that the trade association was planning a dance to take place after he finished his speech. The dancing space was in front of the speaking platform. Just as a nightclub comedian hates "dead space" in front of him, Reagan recognized the problem and resisted. He persuaded the hotel staff to put some tables in that space, with the suggestion they could move them back later.

PODIUM PLACEMENT

Another time, Reagan reportedly went to a hotel hall that was shaped like an oblong "i"—they planned for him to speak from "inside the dot," isolated from his audience. Instead, he had the podium placed in the middle of the room, on the side, where he could see more of the audience.

This past year I traveled to a speaking engagement in Fort Collins, Colorado, and discovered, when I arrived, that there was a wide space in the middle of the Hilton Hotel ballroom for a color guard to march down. I persuaded them to have the soldiers march down the side and had the tables moved toward the center.

A "HOME-COURT" MICROPHONE

When you "case the joint," you want to make it familiar. You must try to be as comfortable in the space as you would be in your own living room. In the movie *Hoosiers*, Gene Hackman plays the coach of the small-town basketball team that amazingly advances to the state finals. In the hours before their big match, the coach took his nervous players to the court on which they would be playing. It was in a huge auditorium.

The coach asked his team, "How high is the basket here?"

"Ten feet," they replied.

"And how wide is the rim?" he asked further.

"Eighteen inches," they answered.

"Right. Just the same as back home. So let's start thinking of this as our home court."

"OWN THE PLACE"

When I first went to the room where Olivia and I would speak in Newport, Rhode Island, she gave me the advice that Ronnie Reagan had given to her. "Olivia, you've got to act as if you own the place, be it a platform or a podium."

"I PAID FOR THIS MICROPHONE"

In 1980, the first Republican presidential primary debate for the upcoming election was held in Manchester, New Hampshire. The Bush people said, "There should be only two debaters, he and Reagan." Reagan, however, invited the other candidates—Bob Dole, Howard Baker, and Jack Kemp. Bush objected. Reagan said to the local debate chairman, "Mr. Green, I paid for this microphone." After the debate, Bush was told by his press aide, Peter Teeley, "Bad news, then the good news. First, Reagan won it all that first moment when he said, 'I paid for the microphone.' The good news is that even though you lost the debate that followed, it didn't matter. The race was already all over."

BIG SPLASH?

And if you own the place, you have to know where the restroom is. Reagan used to quote Churchill's rhyming rule: "Before you speak, take a leak."

While we're on the subject, remember, if you are

hooked up to a wireless microphone, make sure it is turned off before you go to the restroom. In the Broadmoor Hotel in Colorado Springs, Colorado, I forgot about the microphone on me when I flushed. I learned right afterward, to my chagrin, that the loud whooshing sound had resonated throughout the ballroom. It was not the kind of splash I wanted to make with the audience.

Ronald Reagan would not have made that mistake. You may not be president, but you have to manifest the command authority at all times. Once I was speaking to the Texas Association of Realtors in Corpus Christi. I was welcomed royally—picked up by a limousine at the airport and given the hotel's presidential suite, which seemed as big as a basketball court. As I waited to speak, a huge, movie-sized screen flashed portraits first of President Reagan (during the pledge of allegiance), then of Jesus (during the invocation), and then of yours truly (during the introduction, which said, among other extravagant things, that I had been "counselor and adviser to presidents"). I was ten minutes into my talk when a hotel manager came on stage and whispered in my ear that I had to come immediately to the office. It seems my MasterCard account was insufficient. Well, the room was one thousand dollars a night, and even though I was not paying for the room, according to hotel rules, the available balance on your credit card must equal five times the price of the room. I plastered a smile to my face and whispered back that I knew the president of Sheraton (I didn't), and that if he didn't want to be sent to Sheraton-Nome in Alaska, he'd better let me come in and settle it later. Meantime, the thousand realtors in my audience were waiting to find out what was going on. I boomed out, "I don't care whether it's the president of the United States. I will not let my speech to the Texas Realtors be interrupted." It triggered a standing ovation. The point is that you should never let your command authority as a speaker be diminished.

MIC RIGHT?

You do not look like you are in command if your head is jerking from one side to another. On one occasion, I spoke at a Vancouver yacht club from a wide, raised head table in a room that was wide but of short depth. Whenever I turned to my far left or right, I learned later, my voice had not been picked up by the microphone.

One business executive, to whom I was imparting this advice of casing the joint, first replied, "Look, Humes. I'm not deluged with after-dinner speech invitations. Your advice for speeches doesn't really apply to me."

"Maybe not," I replied, "but you will agree that you should check out the microphone and the audio-visual equipment for slides and make sure they work." Have someone stand in the back of the room to find out if he or she can hear you.

One time, as I started my talk, I discovered the microphone was not working. I remarked while engineers were adjusting it, "I'm always nervous about microphones ever since I worked at the Nixon White House."

If you should encounter problems, you might want to say something humorous. If you draw a blank, simply say, "Don't worry. I planned this to build up anticipation."

PANEL POSITION

Would-be speakers should also find out in advance if there are to be other speakers. If you are slated to be number two, sandwiched between the first and third, you may want to call ahead, say that you have to leave early, and ask if you could please speak first. The speaker who leads off faces the most alert and ready-to-listen audience. If you have to go last, the position can be advantageous, since your words are the last thing the audience hears.

Make sure you know who is to introduce you and that he or she has received your résumé material beforehand (by the way, encourage the introducer not to just read the résumé aloud—boring!). Find out who else will speak. In a speech at the Bohemian Grove in California in 1995, I spoke about my experience as a White House speechwriter, including my part in writing the words for the plaque to be left on the moon vehicle in 1969. I did not know that I would be followed by a former astronaut, Charles "Pete" Conrad!

RED-FACED RONNIE

Once, when he was governor of California, Reagan was invited to Mexico City. He failed to find out the exact role of the other dignitaries at the head table.

Reagan delivered his address, which was received by scattered, unenthusiastic applause. Said Reagan later,

> *I was a bit embarrassed, but even more so, when the next speaker, a representative of the Mexican government, spoke in Spanish. He was interrupted at virtually every other line with the most enthusiastic kind of applause. Now I don't understand Spanish, but to hide the fact, I started to clap too. At the end, I clapped longer than any one else, until the American ambassador leaned over to me and said, "I wouldn't do that if I were you. He's interpreting your speech."*

WHO IS THE AUDIENCE, REALLY?

It pays to take the time to call the program chairman beforehand to get an idea of the audience and the occasion.

This writer, when he was in the State Department, was once invited to speak to a chapter of the American Association of University Women in suburban Chicago. In my mind's eye, I pictured then a rough equivalent of the League of Women Voters. When I arrived, I found that in manner and outlook, they were closer to the Daughters of the American Revolution.

Another time when I was asked to speak to a savings and loan league in New Jersey, I expected a group of bankers. But, to my surprise, I found that most of the audience was made up of young girls in their twenties and sporting beehive hairdos. They were being treated by their bosses to a night out at a special festive banquet.

In both cases, if I had taken the time to call ahead and ask about the age and background of the audience, I would have saved myself some grief.

Reagan, as president, made sure he was briefed thoroughly about every audience he would face. In the spring of 1985, the president took a trip to Europe. On this state visit, he was invited to speak to the Lisbon parliament. He had been warned that some Communist members may be attending, and that they may even walk out in protest.

Just as he began his remarks, the Communist members made a show of walking out. Reagan then quipped, "I'm sorry if some of the chairs on the left seem to be uncomfortable."

In 1986, Reagan went to Moscow at the invitation of Chairman Gorbachev. A speech was arranged at Moscow's University. Reagan's humor went over very well, and his allusions to Russian authors like Gogol and Chekhov struck a chord. But the audience sat silent during his argument for a free market economy. Reagan's White House did not know beforehand that the audience had been restricted to Young Communist League members.

SPEECH A SUCCESS—AUDIENCE A FAILURE

On one occasion, when Reagan was on the speaking circuit, his talk did not trigger the invariable rousing applause and standing ovation. Later, his wife, Nancy, asked him about the talk. He answered, "Well, the speech was a success, but the audience was a failure."

Actually, in that case, Reagan had not even been introduced until a quarter to ten. After a ninety-minute cocktail reception, a five-course dinner feast laden with wine, and the presentation of fifty association awards, most of the audience was too tired, sleepy, and full of alcohol to pay attention to his talk.

Reagan would always say that the success of a talk lies not just in the speaker but in the audience. The more alert the audience, the better the response. The more knowledgeable the audience, the better the reception.

This writer once spoke to the Philadelphia Bar Association and the Pennsylvania Bar Association on two separate occasions in the same year. After the second engagement, the association's executive director told me, "Humes, you were good, but you were better when I heard you earlier in Philadelphia. You were in better form."

"You're right. In Philadelphia, I spoke at a luncheon where there was no booze served beforehand or during the meal. And because the attorneys had to get back to the office before two, others at the head table were brief in their remarks. In Harrisburg, there was a long cocktail hour, and each of the officers—outgoing president, incoming president, and program chairman, all felt it was an opportunity to display their forensic skills. I didn't get to speak until 10:15." I concluded with, "I was at my best, but the audience could not be at their best at that late hour."

Reagan once quipped, "I'm here to do a job of speaking—and you to do a job of listening. I hope I finish my job before you do."

Remember, find out at what stage of the event you are supposed to speak and what exactly will be the age and background of the audience.

If you want in your talk to score top points like Ronald Reagan, make sure you have first "cased the joint."

CHAPTER XII

"LIES, DAMNED LIES, AND STATISTICS"

★ ★ ★ ★ ★

Ronald Reagan won just about every political debate in his life. In 1966, the Town Hall Meeting of the Air invited Senator Robert Kennedy to debate Governor Reagan. Kennedy's staff—swallowing their own propaganda that the former actor was a lightweight—eagerly welcomed the invitation to a forum that featured a question-and-answer format that would conclude with addresses by the two respective participants. Kennedy's advisers figured Reagan would surely flounder against the experienced Senator.

"REAGAN CLEANS BOBBY'S CLOCK"

Reagan, however, in Kennedy's own staff's words, "cleaned our clock," and Bobby stormed, "Who's the SOB who set up this engagement?"

In New Hampshire, in February 1980, Reagan knocked George Bush out of the Republican race in their debate in Manchester. In his first debate with President Carter in September of that year, Reagan bested the president by attacking Carter's economic record and went ahead to lead the polls from then to election day.

Just about the only debate he ever lost was his first debate with former vice president Walter Mondale, his Democratic presidential opponent in 1984.

Reagan's staff had been worried by the image the mainstream media was painting that Reagan, at age seventy-seven—by then the oldest president in history—was not quite on top of things. So to counter that, Reagan's aides tried to cram all sorts of statistics into his head—statistics on housing starts, budget items, increasing tax revenues, and declining interest rates.

The outcome was just the opposite of what they had hoped for. He did appear old and a bit befuddled.

"LET REAGAN BE REAGAN"

Reagan's old Californian friends called in and demanded, "Let Reagan be Reagan." The campaign aides did so, and he won. Remember the question of his age. "I'm not going to exploit for political purposes my opponent's youth and inexperience." Even Mondale was floored, letting out a spontaneous laugh. Reagan followed with inspirational stories, not lifeless statistics, to expand on his campaign theme, "Morning in America."

Reagan would agree with Winston Churchill's favorite

Prime Minister, Benjamin Disraeli, who famously said, "There are three kinds of lies—lies, damned lies, and statistics."

"LIES, DAMNED LIES, AND STATISTICS"

Speakers think statistics prove their points, but former presidential speechwriters, like me, believe that numbers often do not tell the whole story, employ a wrong database, or are used out of context. We know that because we have, in attempts to respond to press queries, crafted speeches that are factually correct but do not quite tell the whole picture.

Reagan related a story once that underscored his lack of faith in statistics.

> *A family on their way to Florida stopped at a McDonald's near Myrtle Beach. Their nine-year-old son approached an elderly man in shorts and a Hawaiian sports shirt who was nursing an iced tea.*
>
> *The boy said, "Hello, Mr. Man, where are you from? We live in Ohio."*
>
> *The man disgruntedly replied, "I live here."*
>
> *"That's neat. I'm going to be ten in three weeks. How old are you?"*
>
> *"I'll be eighty next week."*
>
> *"That's really neat. My dad told me that for every eighty-year-old man, there are seven women."*

"Son," the senior citizen replied, "that's the most meaningless statistic I've ever heard."

The first time Reagan voted for a Republican candidate for president was in 1952, for General Eisenhower. After he left the White House in 1961, Eisenhower would spend his winters in Palm Springs, California. There Reagan met the general several times. Reagan was fascinated to learn that when Eisenhower was a major in the 1930s, the former president had once drafted speeches for General Douglas MacArthur in the Philippines, and that he also had written his bestselling book *Crusade in Europe* without the aid of a ghostwriter.

In fact, General Eisenhower told Reagan he owed his rise in the Army bureaucracy to his talents as a writer. After World War I, General Pershing had ordered an account of World War I battles to be written. But when Pershing read the resulting statistic-laden report, which tediously listed the number of casualties on every page, it put him to sleep. So Pershing turned to Eisenhower, at that time a captain, to give it a try. The result was lucid, descriptive prose depicting World War I battles with compelling stories about personal heroism.

SOMNOLENT STATISTICS

Eisenhower did not have to sell Reagan, who was just start-
ing his lecture tours on behalf of General Electric, on the
importance of not boring listeners with statistics.

It is a lesson that would-be speakers should take to heart.
Too many corporate executives, in particular, believe that
profit and production statistics should be accepted like holy
writ. They do not realize that listeners can be as skeptical
of numbers as they are of advertising claims.

But one statistic you can believe in is that nine out of
ten listeners cannot recite the next day one statistic heard
the day before. (Unless, that is, the speaker had put it in the
context of a word picture story to explain it.)

"A TRIP TO THE MOON"

In 1958, President Eisenhower did not like a speech
drafted for him by Kevin McCann about billion-dollar
deficit spending. The litany of statistics was too numbing,
so he said to McCann, "If I took a billion dollars and put
each dollar end to end, would it go to the moon?" McCann
called the Department of Commerce and put a statistician
to work on the measurements. In a speech weeks later,
Eisenhower said this:

To understand the billion-dollar deficit, imagine taking
all the one-dollar bills and laying them out end to end.
Why, it would more than go to the moon and back again.

NUMBING NUMBERS

"Profit centers," "accountability," "quality control," and other phrases that business executives like to bandy about are abstractions that go in and out of the listeners' ears unless they are presented in a word picture. And the most difficult abstraction to etch permanently in the audience's mind is a statistic—a row of numbers.

This writer cannot even remember his license plate number when he registers at a motel, and has to take his card out each time he needs to write his Social Security number on a form.

Statistics, like travel baggage, might be necessary, but they weigh you down and slow you down, too.

Before speaking, Reagan would install a near-sighted lens in his right eye and a far-sighted lens in his left eye—one to read the notes or text before him and the other to look at the audience. Reagan likened statistics to the different contact lenses. Some statistics are cited precisely to obtain immediate credibility; others are framed roundly so they will be remembered by the audience.

If you are obligated to cite statistics in a speech—for example, "We had 173,546 new customers last year"—try to follow them up with something like, "That means we doubled our sales in a year."

Chairman and CEO David Kearns, in a talk on management efficiencies, involved his audience with this statistic picture: "I can see that all the tables seat eight. Well, consider that two of you are going to go back to your office to correct the other six's mistakes."

Reagan, in his talks for General Electric, would attack the class-envy card that pitted poor against the rich. Reagan would tell about a man who once came to Andrew Carnegie, the billionaire steel baron.

> *"Mr. Carnegie, you are the richest man in the world. Don't you think you should share some of your wealth?"*
>
> *"Yes," said Carnegie, surprising the man. Carnegie then sent a note to his male secretary, who appeared in a few moments with a check for the caller in the amount of thirty-two cents. That number was derived by taking Carnegie's wealth of hundreds of millions and dividing it by the population of the world.*

LIMIT AND LIFT

A speech is like a balloon launched into the sky. Statistics are like stones that weigh it down. Too many stones, and the balloon will sink.

THE THREE R'S

Schools, in the olden days, used to feature the three R's. Another kind of three R's are rules for using statistics: reduce, round out, and relate. Limit your statistics to one. Then round out the statistics to a simple ratio—about six out of ten, almost two out of three, more than three out of four. Then tell an anecdote that tells a story of the statistics—"More soldiers died in the Civil War than in all the other wars combined, from World War I, through World War II, all the way up to Iraq."

Too often, speakers treat statistics about their companies' economic prospects like stones—precious gems that confirm and illuminate their speech.

But Nancy Reagan, one of the most fashionable first ladies in history, said too many women undermine their dressing statement by wearing too much jewelry. She would always check the mirror to see if the earrings, bracelet, or necklace was one too many. Limit the statistics and, in doing so, lift your talk.

CHAPTER XIII

ACING THE Q&A

★ ★ ★ ★ ★

In 1969, when college campuses erupted protesting the Vietnam War, leaders from the seven University of California campuses asked to see Governor Reagan in his office in Sacramento.

The delegation arrived in the capital. Most of them were barefoot and wore torn T-shirts. When Governor Reagan entered his office, they were sprawled out on the floor. None of them stood up. Their spokesman said:

> *Governor, we want to hear some answers from you. But we know that it is impossible for you to understand us. How do you plan to say anything meaningful to us? You probably can't even connect with your own children. You weren't raised in a time of instant communications or satellites and computers solving problems that previously took hours, days, or even weeks to solve. You didn't live in an age of space travel and journeys to the moon, of jet travel, or high-speed electronics, so how can you speak to us?*

Reagan listened to their spokesman intently and nodded in appreciation of these words. Then, in a pause, he looked around at the others seated on the floor. Finally, with a big grin, he responded:

> *You're absolutely right. We didn't have those things when we were your age. We invented them.*

LISTEN, PAUSE, GRIN

That was the strategy of Reagan in handling hostile questions: LISTEN, PAUSE, AND GRIN. In kindergarten, we learned to "stop, look, and listen" before crossing a street, because if you do not, a car might hit you.

In the 1976 campaign, President Gerald Ford did not fully listen to a question in his final debate with Jimmy Carter. He did not stop to consider the exact words of the question and give himself time to frame an answer, and it cost him the election. To a question about the Soviets and Eastern Europe, he responded, "Poles don't consider themselves dominated by the Soviet Union." What Ford did was automatically give the answer to a question about Poland that he had rehearsed addressing in preparing for the debate.

Ford violated what his Yale law professors had told him and his classmates. Read the question thoroughly; then, reread it. With only a quick read, the facts might remind you of a case you once read. But closer examination may reveal differences.

One of the major reasons Reagan had decided to run against the incumbent president of his own party was that Ford was such an inarticulate spokesman as the leader of the free world in championing the cause of freedom. Ford's gaffe in the debate proved Reagan right.

Too many executives do not act as if they are concentrating on the question posed. The expression on their faces often says they heard it before. They look impatient. Don't let your expression show a know-it-all look. Even if you have heard it before, act like it is the first time, and that the questioner has really hit on something.

Then pause, as if you are considering the question and all its implications before your answer. It shows you respect your questioner, as well as your audience.

THE INSURANCE PAUSE

What's more, answering an easy question too quickly limits your time in later answering a tough question. I once heard a CEO of a major *Fortune* 500 company field some questions from shareholders. He answered the questions crisply and briskly about future earnings, new products, and a possible merger. But when it came to questions about a new product by a rival company, he stumbled and mumbled with a rambling answer. If he had paused before delivering answers to the earlier and easier questions and had been a little more deliberate in his responses, he would have bought himself more insurance time on the tougher questions.

In the 2008 campaign, Mitt Romney was too quick and pat with some of his answers, such as those about his religion, as if he had memorized them. But he displayed slower and more unsure responses to questions, such as those regarding our trade agreements with China, he obviously had not heard before.

THE QUESTIONER'S GAME OF "GOTCHA"

At a Young Presidents' Organization conference in 1976, Reagan was questioned by three panelists. That was the year Reagan was running against President Ford. One panelist was working for Ford and wanted to show Reagan as being too shallow for the office of president.

To expose Reagan's superficiality, he asked, "What are your thoughts on the intrinsic moral capability of a man?"

In his reply, Reagan did not fall into the trap of answering this theological query, but instead talked about individual responsibility. He then answered some of the other panelists' questions. When the hostile panelist's turn came around again, he said, "Mr. Reagan, I didn't understand your answer."

"Young man," Reagan replied with a smile, "I didn't understand your question." It triggered laughter from the audience.

Remember, Reagan did not scowl and reveal that the unfriendly questioner might have scored in a game of "Gotcha."

Reagan went prepared to press conferences. His speechwriters would figure out the toughest of questions that the Washington press corps might toss at the president, and then draft clever answers to them.

You should be doing the same thing before a talk. For a chamber of commerce address, is there a bond referendum someone may ask you about? Are there rumors that your company might merge or leave town? Just preparing your talk is not enough. Write down beforehand the answers to some possible questions, but do not, of course, take the answers with you to the talk and read them to the audience.

As I've said before, Franklin Roosevelt was Reagan's first political hero. In his reelection campaign in 1940, the AFL-CIO provided most of the money and manpower to finance the campaign and get out the vote. The press was full of articles about the special interest's influence on the president.

ROOSEVELT WAS READY

In the first news conference after his election, a reporter asked, "Mr. President, I suppose you will consult the powerful interests that control you before making your cabinet selection."

"Young man," Roosevelt snapped back in mock protest, "I would ask you keep my wife's name out of it."

During the Civil War, Lincoln's Radical Republican opponents in Congress were taking the country right to hell. Senator Ben Wade led a delegation to the White House to register their complaints to the president. "Mr. President," said Wade, "this administration is going right to perdition. Why, it's only a mile away from hell right now."

Lincoln replied, "Well, Senator, that's just about the distance from the White House to Capitol Hill."

FRANKLIN WAS READY

When Benjamin Franklin was our minister to France during the Revolutionary War, his principal for persuasion was King Louis XVI. Franklin needed his assent for any recognition or loan to the beleaguered colonies. It was known that the king was hesitant to side with an attempt to overthrow a monarch, even if it was the British. Secondly, he did not think the colonies were strong enough to beat the British. The king was reluctant to give an audience to Franklin.

But there was to be a ball at Versailles that the King would be attending. Knowing the Bourbon King's taste in women ran to the bosomy and fleshy, Franklin deliberately took as his guest a thin and bony mademoiselle. After Franklin presented himself and his partner to the king, Louis took Franklin aside and whispered, "Franklin, why did you choose her? The lady does not do justice to her décolletage." Franklin had his answer prepared. "Yes, Sire, she suffers from the same problem as our Continental Congress—an uncovered deficit. But unlike the lady in question, your loan will cover that deficit and make the winning difference." Franklin got the massive loan.

John F. Kennedy was the first president to appoint a close relative to a cabinet post when he named his brother, Bobby, Attorney General. JFK deflected any questioning of his decision with wit: "I thought I should give Bobby a little experience before he went to practice law."

When I was working with former President Ford in Vail, Colorado, in 1977 on his autobiography, *A Time to Heal*, Robert Pierpoint of CBS News was flying out for a taped interview with the former chief executive.

In preparing for it, Ford told me, "I know one question he's sure to ask. Carter announced last week that he's cutting the White House staff by fifteen percent. Now, you and I know that he hasn't cut it at all," he continued. "He's just having their salaries picked up by the agricultural and interior departments."

So I prepared this answer:

> *When Herbert Hoover followed Calvin Coolidge as president in 1929, the new chief executive did away with the riding horses and stables at the White House.*
>
> *When reporters asked Coolidge in Plymouth, Vermont, his reaction to the executive decision, Coolidge answered, "Where are they feeding the horses now, Fort Myers?*

In other words, the horses will still be on the government roster.

Unfortunately, Ford blew it when Pierpoint asked the anticipated question. Ford said, "Jamie Humes tells the great story about Coolidge and Hoover…"

He should not have mentioned my name. I was a nobody, and so they did not use Ford's answer.

For George H.W. Bush's last debate with Governor Michael Dukakis in 1988, we all knew that the unhappy Iran-Contra episode in the last years of Reagan's presidency would be brought up for Bush to defend, since he had, after all, been vice president.

Bush's answer was prepared in advance: "I'll take half the responsibility for any of President Reagan's mistakes if you give me half the credit for his accomplishments."

Winston Churchill used to spend two hours on every paragraph of a speech. For Question Time in the House of Commons, he would also prepare assiduously.

When Churchill returned to 10 Downing Street in October 1951, he began to abolish some of the Socialist programs of the past six years. If and when the Labourite opposition attacked capitalism as fostering "inequality" in Britain, he had his answer ready, and he soon had opportunity to respond to such a charge:

> *I must agree with the learned young member. Conservatism does promote inequality, whereas your socialism does increase equality—the equality of misery and poverty, but I much prefer the unequality of wealth and conservatism.*

Ronald Reagan did not like to be open for questions after a talk. On the speech circuit, he liked to leave his audience on an emotional high. The question-and-answer session that followed, he figured, would be anticlimactic. Of course, in touring General Electric plants, he had to be ready to field questions from employees. Not until he ran for governor in 1962 did he first face hostile questions. And he developed a strategy for meeting them.

INSULATE

First, he would insulate himself from the impact of the question. A bank vice president whom I once heard speak in a neighborhood forum began the process of insulating himself when he fielded a version of a "beating your wife" question. A representative from a community action group asked,

> *"When are you going to stop jacking up mortgage prices so high that poor people can't buy houses?"*
> *The banker listened intently and patiently to the hostile question, then turned toward the other side of the audience. "The question concerns the establishment of mortgage rates in order to ensure that those with marginal security credit do not have their houses repossessed."*

RESTATE

The technique, which Reagan practiced, is seen as a courtesy to make sure the entire audience understands the question, but it also serves to cool off the hot, aggressive tone of the question.

An immediate answer from the banker would have triggered the direct and personal confrontation of a two-man argument. Instead, he depersonalized the potentially nasty situation into an opportunity for group discussion. By reflecting the question, he diffused the tension while giving himself time to think of a good answer.

ARTICULATE

> *When farmers raise the price of butter, the supermarkets that buy the butter also have to increase their prices. Similarly, banks get their money from the government. When the Federal Reserve Board raises its discount rate, we have to raise the cost of borrowing to the mortgage seeker because our cost of borrowing money is higher.*

The audience was generally satisfied with the banker's answer, but the hostile questioner tried to ask another question. The banker refused to be drawn into a two-man shouting match that would only degrade his stature and demean his authority. He wisely called upon someone else.

That was also the technique of Reagan who, in the White House, refused to allow follow-up questions from the same reporter. The rest of the Washington press corps went along with this rule, because they resented anyone who tried to monopolize the question period.

DEPERSONALIZE

In the neighborhood meeting, the banker found the next question was just as hostile.

> *When are the banks going to stop picking up the discounted commercial paper of those fly-by-night operations that cheat poor people when they sell them shoddy refrigerators and ovens?*

Again the banker depersonalized the question by repeating it and rephrasing it to another part of the room, but he also "dissected" the question.

DISSECT

The question about installment purchases of refrigerators and other home appliances, the banker said, is really two questions.

> *First, should you prevent those stores from selling washing machines or TV sets to people who are so hard up that they couldn't get a loan to buy them at a bank? The answer is that even if you wanted to, you couldn't. It is not possible to stop people from buying what they want, even if they do not have the money. It would be like stopping them from spending their paychecks on liquor or gambling.*

Now the second question involved bank notes. Notes are a form of money. We could not check the individual history of each fifty-dollar bill we receive. If we tried to, the whole banking system would shut down. So the answer is not in reforming the banks but in reforming the consumer laws and educating the public.

In his recent campaign for president, Governor Romney was asked, "Do you think your Mormon religion, which is anti-Jew, good politics for winning the Republican presidential nomination?" He managed to direct it back in the best light:

The question carries the false assumption that I am anti-Israel, when just the opposite is true. I have visited Israel; and I believe the Jewish community in Massachusetts will tell you, there has been no more staunch a defender of its security. Yes, I am a Mormon, but that does not mean I oppose Jewish values. We Mormons respect Jewish and Christian values.

"ONE MAGIC PHRASE"

In December 1984, a group called Citizens for America, a pro-Reagan group of conservative activists, visited the White House to hear many Cabinet officers speak and to have a photograph session with the president.

I heard one future candidate for Congress say, "Mr. President, what is the single most important advice you can give me?"

Replied Reagan, "Let me give you one magic phrase to use in response if you are asked a question about which you know little or nothing—and you're going to be asked a lot of those questions: 'I don't know, but I sure as heck am going to find out.'"

A top executive of a prominent investment bank institution was giving a talk to financial planners. He was going to deliver his entire presentation with a series of slides, but an experienced communication adviser counseled him to do an opening and closing with slides and explanations in between. Because he talked conversationally about the company he knew from top-to-bottom, he was both warm and winning. When he finished his closing remarks, he opened the floor to questions. He fielded the first few well, but then an audience member asked about a development he had never heard of before. The executive shook his head and replied, "How the hell did you ever come up with that one? I promise I'm going to find out, but in the meantime, someone in the audience may have the answer."

One did, and the executive applauded. He walked out of the meeting with cheers. He had sold the audience on both himself and the company he represented.

To any question Reagan always made a point to listen closely. Then he would pause to allow himself to frame the best response and then, with a smile, would deliver.

But if he spotted a hostile or aggressive question, he would shift into his 4 Ds mode. Ron's rule for answering a hostile question was to *delay*, *depersonalize*, *dissect*, and *deflect*.

THE 4 D'S

Delay the impact of the nasty query by repeating it not to the questioner but to another part of the audience.

Depersonalize the question by rephrasing it in a neutral way.

Dissect the question by breaking it into parts or by extracting the unfair assumption.

Deflect the question by giving a response to your rephrasing of it.

Remember, you do not have to hit it out of the park. Just try to make contact, hit safely, and do so like Reagan—with a smile, not a frown.

CHAPTER XIV

BREVITY IS BEAUTY

★ ★ ★ ★ ★

One of Reagan's favorite stories was about the shortest and best sermon he had ever heard. He was a ten-year-old boy in Dixon, Illinois, in 1921, and his mother, Nell Reagan, would take him and his brother, "Moon," to the Christian Church. "One Sunday, it was so hot," Reagan said, "that you could have fried an egg on the stone steps up to the wooden white church." As the three sweltered during the service, "Dutch," as he was then called, was dreading the upcoming long sermon. When the preacher stepped up to the pulpit, he simply pointed down and said, "It's hotter down there." Reagan later said it was the briefest and best sermon he ever heard.

"BREVITY, THE SOUL OF WIT"

Reagan agreed with the Bard who wrote, "Brevity is the soul of wit." Reagan told this sermon anecdote to the retired General Eisenhower in Palm Springs in the 1960s, and Ike, in turn, related it in an appearance he made to U.S. troops in England just before D-Day. It was April 1944. The field was sodden with spring rains. He arrived at the

Norfolk encampment. Thousands of troops stood ramrod stiff awaiting remarks by the supreme allied commander.

As Eisenhower advanced, he slipped on the wet ground and fell flat on his ass. Not a blink of a reaction was noted in the troops standing in stiff military attention. Ike got up, wiped off his backside, and then, with both arms raised in a victory salute, unleashed a huge guffaw. The soldiers erupted in gales of laughter. To their applause, Eisenhower walked away without saying a word. He later told Reagan it was the best morale-boosting appearance he made in the whole war.

INCISIVE SOUNDS DECISIVE

Knowing when to keep your remarks short or even when to say nothing at all is the sign of a confident and poised executive. Remember what the notoriously long-winded former Vice President Hubert Horatio Humphrey was once told by his wife, Muriel: "To be immortal, you don't have to be eternal." Bill Clinton learned that lesson when his stem-winder keynote speech bombed at the Democratic National Convention in 1992.

In the 1960s, Reagan, as a spokesman for General Electric, made speeches across the country, including many appearances at company plants. In Owensboro, Kentucky, he faced some five thousand women—General Electric's "ladies in white." They were called that because they wore sterile nylon gowns and caps as they made electronic tubes.

One woman greeted him and asked, "How do you like Owensboro?"

"Fine," answered Reagan. "How can I complain about being here with five thousand girls? Just think, next week I'm in Pittsfield, Massachusetts, where there are thirteen thousand men."

Another woman in the crowd yelled out, "Why don't you stay here, and we'll go to Pittsfield?" The "women in white" broke out in gales of laughter. The former movie actor, Reagan, dropped the idea of giving them a talk and went out to shake the lady's hand and to greet others milling around her.

THE BEST SPEECH CAN BE NO SPEECH

Great speakers like Reagan and Eisenhower knew to quit when they were ahead. They sensed whether to abbreviate or abort any talk. It's the wannabe great speakers who feel compelled to use every allotted minute, and then some, on the podium.

In 1786, George Washington was offered the floor for a speech after he was elected the presiding officer at the Constitutional Convention. He delivered one sentence: "Let us raise a standard to which the wise and honest can repair."

SHORTER IS SWEETER

After he took office, Reagan arranged for the portrait of the terse and tax-cutting Calvin Coolidge to be brought out from the White House sub-basement and restored to display in a prominent place.

As an admonition to wordy aides in their presentations, Reagan would tell them of the time "Silent Cal" was approached by a woman who said, "Mr. President, I bet my husband I could get you to say more than two words."

"You lose," was Coolidge's reply.

FOUR PROMISES AND FOUR MINUTES

Harry Truman surprised Winston Churchill by telling him that James Polk was his favorite president. Polk was inaugurated in 1845. The Democrats, regaining control for the first time in four years, gathered to listen to his inaugural address. Four years earlier, Whig President William Henry Harrison had spoken for three hours, and the attendees expected no less from Polk. Instead, he spoke for about four minutes. He promised to annex Texas, abolish the National Bank, lower the tariff, and settle the Oregon boundary dispute with Great Britain. Then he sat down. In history books, his inaugural is often considered the greatest—at least, to those who measure it by results. Polk followed through and fulfilled all four things he had promised.

"YOU DON'T HAVE TO EAT THE WHOLE THING"

In the upstairs bathroom, my wife has this saying in big gothic print framed over the scale: "YOU DON'T HAVE TO EAT THE WHOLE THING!" It is an everyday admonition to her portly spouse, her way of telling me that just because there is a glob of mashed potatoes or a slice of roast beef on my plate doesn't mean I have to wipe the plate clean. But some executives believe that if they do not use every second of their allotted time, it is like paying for five minutes of radio advertisement and speaking for only four and a half minutes.

"LESS IS MORE"

"Less is more" is a maxim that has been identified with both architecture and fashion.

What is the greatest speech ever delivered? Many would argue it was Lincoln's Gettysburg Address. The featured orator of the day, Edward Everett, spoke for two hours. Then President Lincoln followed with his two-minute gem. (Its brevity, as well as its beauty, has made it the most memorized speech in all of American history.)

BRIEF IS BETTER; SHORT IS SHARPER

"Lincoln's address," Reagan said once, "only contained 266 words." Then he added, "The Ten Commandments has

297 words, the Declaration of Independence has only 309 words, and the Lord's Prayer has just fifty-seven words. Compare that to the agricultural department order setting the price of cabbage—26,411 words."

Reagan also used to tell about the time Prime Minister Churchill went back to his old school, Harrow, during World War II. The headmaster made a tedious and long introduction, trying to include all the many accomplishments of this most famous old Harrovian.

When Churchill rose to speak, he gave the students a one-sentence speech they would remember all their lives. "Never, never, never, never, never, never give in, except to dictates of honor and good sense."

Listening to a long speech is like reading a book without punctuation. General Eisenhower, while president of Columbia University, found himself on one occasion following the talks of three preceding panelists. When it was Eisenhower's turn, at about 10:30 that night, he declared, "Every article or speech needs punctuation. Tonight I am the punctuation—the period." And he sat down.

Who was the most remembered speaker on that panel that evening? Who did the audience go home talking about?

Surveys show that where there is an array of speakers, the one who speaks the longest is remembered the least.

TERSE TRIUMPHS OVER THE TEDIOUS

The first political speech I remember was one I heard when my father was running for judge in 1938. His opponent gave a forty-minute treatise on jurisprudence and closed with, "I ask all of you to vote for Charles Beidelspacher on November 4."

My father got up and said, "I hope all of you on November 4 will vote for my good friend, Charlie Beidelspacher, but on November 6, Election Day, vote for Sam Humes." To resounding cheers, he sat down. Come November 6, he won the election.

ONE-SENTENCE TALK

Taking a page from my father's book, I delivered this one-sentence talk in Williamsport, Pennsylvania, when running against an incumbent legislator at age twenty-six. Though I had been born in Williamsport, I had not lived there for close to twenty years. I had moved from Washington, where I had just finished law school, and then rented an apartment in Williamsport and announced my candidacy. At a joint appearance before a big women's group, my opponent, for fifteen minutes, attacked me for being a carpet-bagger and not owning any property.

When it came my turn, I reached into my briefcase and

pulled out a large, folded white sheet and said, "Ladies, here is the deed for Wildwood Cemetery, where four generations of my family rest—and so, God willing, will this fifth generation."

One of Reagan's most historic lines came in Berlin in 1987. Reagan followed Soviet leader Mikhail Gorbachev, who delivered a forty-minute talk on his reforms of *glasnost* and *perestroika*. Reagan was brief with short remarks but closed with a challenge. "General Secretary Gorbachev, if you seek peace, if you seek prosperity for the Soviet Union and Eastern Europe, if you seek liberalization, come here to this gate! Mr. Gorbachev, open this gate. Mr. Gorbachev, tear down this wall!"

BRIEF IS BETTER

The persuasive power of a talk is measured by its impact. No rambler in an ambling talk comes off as a leader.

Remember, brief is better. Short is sharper.

CHAPTER XV

"SELLIN' IS BELIEVIN'"

★ ★ ★ ★ ★

Ronald Reagan's final film role was a flop. It was in *The Killers*, 1964, and Reagan, against his own better judgment, played a contract hit man. A glowering and scowling Ronald Reagan did not find audience approval.

Reagan had been told it would be a challenge to play against character. Later he said, "I think the viewers kept waiting for me to repent and become the good guy I usually was in the end."

When in 1978 Gregory Peck played a Nazi doctor in *The Boys from Brazil*, Reagan thought that Peck, the 1962 hero of *To Kill a Mockingbird*, had made a career mistake.

Reagan started out in B movies, where he was often a star reporter uncovering a big city scandal. ("I got a scoop that will break this city wide open.") He always played the "good guy" and yearned for the leading roles his friend and fellow Republican Jimmy Stewart got, such as those in *Mr. Smith Goes to Washington* or *The Man Who Shot Liberty Valance*.

YOU HAVE TO BE YOURSELF

President Lyndon Johnson didn't act himself when he tried to be like Charles de Gaulle when he addressed the nation on television. Privately, however, he was very persuasive when he spoke one-on-one to legislators in the Oval Office.

Richard Nixon was advised by a top communications adviser, Dorothy Sarnoff, to gesture with his hands. The gestures were typed into the scripts of his speeches in brackets, i.e., [point with finger]. Invariably, when Nixon would use each gesture indicated, he was a split second off.

Reagan said, "If you don't use gestures while speaking, don't mess with them at the podium."

"HE MUST HIMSELF BELIEVE"

In advising this writer on speeches, Reagan quoted to me something Churchill had said:

> *Before the speaker can inspire with any emotion, he must be swayed by it himself. To convince them he must himself believe. He is never insincere.*

And a speaker cannot manufacture "sincerity" as Senator Joe Biden tried to do by repeating the phrase "I sincerely believe" in his abortive 2008 campaign.

In the White House, Reagan would not ask protectionists like Pat Buchanan to write a speech for him on free trade. Neither would he direct a staff writer whose wife was pro-choice on the abortion issue to write a pro-life address.

In 1972, President Nixon asked Governor Reagan, the hero of the Republican Party's conservative wing, to deliver some speeches defending the president's historic trip to Beijing to open up relations with the People's Republic of China. The governor dutifully complied, but he did not feel that, as a long-time staunch supporter of Chiang Kai-shek, he was persuasive or eloquent.

Reagan's political soul mate, Margaret Thatcher, would react viscerally when aides would try to put words in her mouth that did not sound like her. In 1979, I was asked by the Conservative Party's Central Office to draft a talk for Thatcher, who had only recently been elected head of the Conservative Party and Leader of the Opposition. The Prime Minister at that time was Labourite Jim Callaghan, an avuncular and warm figure who came off like the proprietor of a London pub. In contrast, Thatcher appeared hard-edged and snappish, even though the Conservative Party at that time was more popular than the incumbent Labourite.

I was asked to draft a speech that emphasized her role as a mother of two, alarmed at the rising cost of milk, eggs, and nappies [diapers].

Accordingly, I wrote a folksy address laced with some gibes at rising costs.

I then met with Mrs. Thatcher at a lunch. She threw the text at me, saying, "Did you ever read Friedrich Hayek's *Road to Serfdom*?"

"Yes," I replied.

"Well, you would not know it by this talk." Margaret Thatcher, who once famously asserted, "This lady's not for turning," would not take the advice of pollsters and focus groups to go folksy.

One reason politicians are held in the lowest esteem is that they will often take on new roles like women do hairstyles. Lawyers are also mistrusted because they, in their advocacy roles, continually and deliberately misstate, disassemble, and lie. And any time a lawyer says, "I want to be honest with you," he is probably being as dishonest as a used car salesman.

In 1992, Governor Clinton, while running against President Bush, said that foreign policy experience should not be the main factor in choosing a president. But then in 2008, when his wife was running against Barack Obama, he inveighed against Obama's lack of experience in national security matters. It is such reversals of opinion that make people distrust politicians.

Attorneys who, as prosecutors, regularly ask for the maximum sentences against criminals use different arguments when they leave the prosecution side and become defense lawyers in private firms. When Abraham Lincoln was asked if he would correct his mistakes, he said, "Yes, a big one, but not a small one." Then they asked for an example of a small one. "Well," replied Lincoln, "I once said 'liar' when I meant to say 'lawyer.'"

Of course, it was once said that actors did "lie" when they played roles. In fact, in seventeenth-century England, the Puritans banned acting in the time of Cromwell. Yet, as Reagan said about his decision to act in *The Killers*, he should not have taken a role in which he, himself, did not believe.

"BE SOLD BEFORE YOU SELL"

If the would-be speaker is not quite sold on a presentation of a new product, he or she should study up on it until thoroughly convinced.

Years ago, one of my first jobs was as legislative counsel for the Greater Philadelphia Chamber of Commerce. Part of that job was to call on companies to sell corporate memberships. I failed to sign up many. So I went back and did some research on specific cases where the chamber of commerce had rendered some special service to a company or had helped them out on a specific problem.

Armed with that information, my presentation for becoming a member was far more enthusiastic and convincing, and I enrolled many companies.

NO LEADER CAN BE LUKEWARM

In October 1964, I was witness to the damage done to a speaker who is mechanical and just goes through the motions. I was running for reelection as a Pennsylvania state legislator. At a Republican dinner in Williamsport—from which I was a state representative—Pennsylvania Lieutenant Governor Ray Shafer was the featured speaker. Senator Barry Goldwater was the Republican candidate currently running against President Lyndon Johnson.

Most Republicans knew that Goldwater's chances of besting the incumbent president were slim-to-none. Still, the Arizona senator had inspired a fervent and devoted cadre of conservative Republicans.

Those Goldwaterites were alienated by Shafer's tepid endorsement. He should have started off with a frank admission that he, like many Pennsylvanians, had supported Pennsylvania Governor Scranton in his failed presidential bid, and then he should have gone on to praise Goldwater's obvious virtues compared to LBJ. He should have said something like this:

> *It is no secret that most of us in Harrisburg and across*
> *this state supported our great Governor Bill Scranton for*
> *the presidential nomination in San Francisco.*
>
> *But that's all over. We are now all united behind*
> *Senator Goldwater. He is as rock-hard in principles as*
> *the Rockies that rise in his native West. He is as straight*
> *as the horse he rides across his ranch. Compare him to*
> *that wheeler-dealer we have now in the White House.*
> *Remember, if you vote for integrity, you'll never regret it.*

Other times, the principal reason speakers are not successful is that they do not know enough about the subject.

One way to build confidence in yourself before a speech is to know more about the subject than anyone else who will be in the audience. In smaller cities and communities, service clubs, chambers of commence, and civic associations are constantly seeking speakers. Sometimes they have seasonal concerns to address—Heart in February, Library Day in April [Shakespeare's birthday], Citizenship in September [Constitution]. If you are asked to speak at one of these occasions, make sure you have expertise in the area.

A broker friend was asked to talk one January to his local chamber of commerce about the economic prospects for the coming year. I advised him to narrow his speech to his expertise in stocks—even more specifically, pharmaceuticals.

A teacher who had just returned from a visit to China once asked me to help her with a twenty-minute talk to a chapter of a university women's organization. She said she wanted to talk about China. "You're going to cover China in twenty minutes?" I challenged her. I then counseled her to concentrate on a specific topic, such as public schools in China—"Better yet," I said, "first grade in China."

Remember, you have maximum leverage at the time the program chairman calls on you and invites you to speak. There is no rule that you must talk about a topic that is chosen for you. Speak about what you know and what excites you.

A speech is not like a diving contest where you are given points for "degree of difficulty." After the talk, listeners do not say, "He did well considering…" They just remember whether or not you did well. Stick to a topic on which you are an expert—your specialty in business, not just real estate, but maybe commercial real estate. In law, are you in estate work or domestic relations? Whole talks can be delivered on wills or prenuptial contracts. Or speak on your favorite hobby, and your enthusiasm can be contagious to your audience. Whatever the occasion, talk only about something you really believe in, with confidence that what you say can make a difference in lives.

"WHO AM I TO CRITICIZE THE WORDS OF THE MASTER…"

One time this writer, after he left the White House, was invited to speak to a New York bankers' association in Albany. I was under the impression that my topic would be "Confessions of a White House Ghost Writer." But then I looked at the title on the announcement bulletin board by the elevator: "Future Trends of Banking" by James C. Humes, former White House Aide. The association had given the title to promote maximum attendance. I began with this story:

> *When I attended Williams College, the most popular course with the football players was "Survey of the New Testament." The reason was the professor, a retired clergyman, gave the same final exam question every year: "Trace and delineate the travels of the Apostle Paul." But in my year, the question asked was, "Analyze and criticize the sermon on the Mount." I witnessed Tiny, a center on the team, whose nickname belied his size.*
>
> *Amazingly, after we returned from the holidays, I heard Tiny got a B+. I asked him what he wrote. "Well, Humes, I wrote, 'Who am I to criticize the words of the Master, but I would like to write about the travels of the Apostle Paul.'"*

Then I added, "Who am I to analyze the future of banking to bankers? But I would like to talk about my experiences as a White House speechwriter." (By the way, feel free to adopt this story as your own if you ever need to extricate yourself from a similar problem.)

To win an audience or a sale, you have to believe in the product you are promoting. If you do not have that enthusiasm, do some research on some unique features or qualities that will ignite that enthusiasm.

Reagan used to spin off a story about a clothing-store salesman.

> *The young man was told that if he was to keep his job he had to unload this sports coat. The garish jacket was something no horse would wear. But he did his homework, and he saw his opportunity when a guy with dark glasses and a dog entered the store.*
>
> *"Sir," the salesman began his spiel, "this tweed jacket was the winner in the Highlands Market Festival. Just feel that Harris tweed. It was woven by an Orkney Island woman of three generations of weavers, from prized sheep, the Cheviots. It has in it strands of the purple heather, the orange of a Scottish sunset, and the blue of the North Sea…"*
>
> *The new owner of the coat walked out of the store. The store boss came out and said, "Did you sell it?"*

The young salesman, who had cuts on his hands, scratches on his face, and tears in his trousers, nodded. "Yes."

"Did he like it?"

"He did, but not that seeing-eye dog of his!"

If seeing is believing, the dog did not believe.

"SELLIN' IS BELIEVIN'"

In 1981, President Reagan was fighting for his life in George Washington University Hospital after his attempted assassination at the Hilton Hotel. Oxygen tanks with tubes attached to his nose were beside his bed. He said to the nurse: "Why can't you get me some good Los Angeles air—air you can see!"

Seein' is believin'. Well, in speaking, "Sellin' is believin'."

In September 1986, President Reagan journeyed to Iceland for a summit conference with Soviet Chairman Mikhail Gorbachev. It was the first high-level negotiation with the two superpowers in seven years. Expectations were high. The new Soviet leader, with his programs of *glasnost* and *perestroika*, seemed to signal new signs of accommodation by Russia. It was almost assumed that a treaty limiting missiles would be signed.

Upon his arrival in Reykjavik, President Reagan and

Secretary of State George Schultz found their Soviet counterparts in a conciliatory mood.

But in the draft of the treaty, the United States had to abandon its Strategic Defense Initiative (SDI), a billion-dollar program the mainstream media had ridiculed as "Star Wars."

"Mr. Chairman, if you are willing to abolish nuclear weapons, why are you so anxious to get rid of a defense against nuclear weapons?" The Soviets remained adamant: "No SDI or no treaty."

Reagan turned to Schultz and said that he could not sign on to something he did not believe was right. "Let's get out of here. George, we're leaving."

The American media, as well as the diplomatic world, was shocked at Reagan's rejection of the peace offer.

The host country, Iceland, the first signatory of NATO, applauded. More than a hundred students from Iceland University came to see the departure of Air Force One and serenaded Reagan with "God Bless America."

Reagan could not sell a treaty to the United States that he did not believe in.

Years later, Gorbachev said that was when he knew the Soviet Union had lost the Cold War.

TEN TIPS TO
SPEAK LIKE REAGAN

★ ★ ★ ★ ★

I. Speak only on what you believe and really care about.

II. Always prepare, revise, and rehearse.

III. Do not lecture to but converse with your audience.

IV. Sell your message with stories not statistics.

V. Do not let your talk turn into a series of introductions to slides.

VI. Never read a speech from a text written like an article.

VII. Always maintain eye contact with the audience, and do not look down while reading text.

VIII. Poke fun at yourself with humor.

IX. Shorter is sharper, and brief is better.

X. End inspirationally by striking chords of pride or hope or love of country or community.

ABOUT THE AUTHOR

James C. Humes has been a lawyer, actor, diplomat, author, and historian. He drafted speeches for five American presidents. He served as White House speechwriter for Nixon and Ford and assisted Ford in the writing of his memoir *A Time to Heal*. He also drafted remarks for Eisenhower, Reagan, and the first President Bush. In addition to being nominated for a Pulitzer Prize, he has written thirty-one books, including *Speak Like Churchill, Stand Like Lincoln*, and *The Wit & Wisdom of Ronald Reagan*. He was a former Woodrow Wilson Fellow at the International Center for Scholars at the Smithsonian. Professor Humes is currently the Schuck Fellow for the Study of Statecraft at the University of Colorado at Colorado Springs.